A UNIVERSAL ETHICAL CLASSIC

THIRUKKURAL

Time, Civilization, and Humanity

திருக்குறள்

காலம், நாகரிகம், மற்றும் மனிதம்

மனிதகுலத்தின் பொதுவான நெறிமுறை நூல்

AUTHOR

Perumal Pugazhendhi, *Ph.D.*

The Universal Ethical Classic of Humanity

Thirukkural:
Time, Civilization, and Humanity

திருக்குறள்:
காலம், நாகரிகம், மற்றும் மனிதம்

மனிதகுலத்தின் பொதுவான நெறிமுறை நூல்

The Universal Ethical Classic of Humanity

ஆசிரியர்: பெருமாள் புகழேந்தி, Ph.D.

மொழியாக்க குறிப்பு — Note on Translation

This book follows the principles outlined below, incorporating seven major scholarly enhancements that transform it into a definitive contemporary study of the *Thirukkural*. By integrating classical commentaries, historical context, comparative philosophy, modern scientific perspectives, and global ethical relevance, the work seeks to present the *Thirukkural* as a timeless guide for humanity in the twenty-first century.

- *பொதுவழக்கு தமிழ்* (Common Tamil): Written in accessible Tamil understood by all readers across generations.
- *பாலினச் சமத்துவம்* (Gender Neutrality): Uses "*அவர்கள்*" and "*ஒருவர்*" instead of gendered pronouns throughout.
- Trilingual Format: Every kural appears with original Tamil, transliteration, and English translation.
- Classical Commentaries: Parimelazhagar, Manakkudavar, Kalingar, and Parithiyar interpretations are included.
- Comparative Philosophy: Connections to Aristotle, Confucius, Buddha, Kant, and Stoicism throughout.
- Modern Relevance: AI Ethics, Climate Science, Corporate Governance, Educational Psychology integrated.
- Full Scholarly References: 20+ page bibliography with primary and secondary sources.

திருவள்ளுவர் இயற்றிய திருக்குறள் 2,000 ஆண்டுகளுக்கும் மேலாக எல்லா மக்களையும் வழிநடத்தி வருகிறது. இந்த நூல் அந்த மகத்தான கருத்துக்களை நவீன ஆய்வு முறைகளுடன் இணைத்து உலக வாசகருக்கு வழங்குகிறது.

Table of Contents

Preface

Part IV — Porul (Society, Governance, and Public Life)

Part V — Inbam (Love)

முன்னுரை — Preface

Why Another Book on Thirukkural?

No work in human history has achieved what Thirukkural has achieved. For more than two thousand years, in just 1,330 two-line verses, each containing exactly seven words, Thiruvalluvar has addressed the deepest dimensions of human life — ethics, governance, and love — transcending time, place, religion, and gender.

Yet most people know Thirukkural only through isolated verses quoted in conversation. Very few understand the complete philosophical architecture of these 133 chapters as an integrated, unified system of thought. This book aims to give that vision to readers of every background — in Tamil and English — combining classical scholarship with contemporary global analysis.

The enhanced edition you hold incorporates seven major scholarly improvements: deeper analytical depth with classical commentary layers, comprehensive scholarly references, trilingual format for every kural, comparative civilization analysis, infographic frameworks, a grand final chapter on global relevance, and substantially expanded modern application chapters.

> *"The greatness of Thirukkural is not that it belongs to Tamil civilization. The greatness of Thirukkural is that it transcends Tamil civilization and speaks to humanity itself."*
> **— Dr. Perumal Pugazhendhi**

Aim, Method, and Audience

This book operates on multiple registers: literary criticism, intellectual history, comparative philosophy, and practical guidance. It addresses: Tamil literary and South Asian civilization scholars, students of philosophy and comparative ethics, governance and leadership professionals, global readers seeking to understand one of humanity's great intellectual achievements, and anyone grappling with 21st century challenges of AI, climate, and global ethics.

பகுதி 1 — PART I

திருவள்ளுவர் மற்றும் அவரது உலகம்

Thiruvalluvar and His World

Chapter 1: Why is the Thirukkural Still Relevant?

No work in world literature has remained as continuously relevant as Thirukkural. Written by the timeless genius Thiruvalluvar, this eternal text contains in just 1,330 kurals virtually every dimension of human life — ethics, governance, education, wealth, friendship, self-discipline, compassion, and love.

Empires rose and fell. Religions crossed continents. Scientific discoveries have transformed civilizations. But the fundamental questions of human existence remain unchanged:

- How should we live with one another?
- What makes a good leader?
- How should wealth be earned and used?
- What is true friendship?
- What is the foundation of a just society?
- How do we find human happiness and fulfillment?

The enduring power of Thirukkural lies in its ability to answer these questions with remarkable clarity and economy of expression — in two lines of seven words each. This is the great gift of Thiruvalluvar to humanity.

குறள் 1 | Kural 1

அகர முதல எழுத்தெல்லாம் ஆதி பகவன் முதற்றே உலகு.

Akara mudala ezhuttellam Aadhi Bhagavan mudatre ulagu.

Translation: *As the letter "A" is the beginning of all letters, so the primal God is the beginning of all creation.*

Commentary: This opening kural establishes the primacy of first principles. Parimelazhagar interprets "Aadhi Bhagavan" as the universal ground of being — not sectarian, but cosmological. Manakkudavar emphasizes the logical structure: just as linguistic meaning depends on foundations, all human flourishing depends on ethical foundations. Philosophically parallel to Aristotle's "unmoved mover" and the Buddhist concept of primordial mind.

குறள் 34 | Kural 34

மனத்துக்கண் மாசிலன் ஆதல் அனைத்தறன் ஆகுல நீர பிற.

Manathukkan maasilaan aadhal anaintaran aagula neer pira.

Translation: *Mental purity is the foundation of all virtue; all else is of no account compared to this.*

Commentary: Parimelazhagar: Virtue begins in the mind before manifesting in action. Manakkudavar: The mind is the wellspring from which ethical conduct emerges. Kalingar: Without inner purity, outer virtue is performance. Modern Psychology: Moral cognition research (Jonathan Haidt, Harvard) confirms that ethical action originates from internal mental frameworks, not merely social conditioning. AI Ethics parallel: A system's values must be aligned internally — not just behaviorally constrained.

The Four Classical Commentators: A Deep Dive

Commentator	Period	Key Focus	Philosophical Stance
Manakkudavar	9th–10th c. CE	Literal clarity, linguistic structure	Empirical, practical ethics
Parithiyar	10th–11th c. CE	Practical moral application	Social ethics, conduct
Kalingar	11th–12th c. CE	Linguistic nuance, layered meaning	Philosophical depth
Parimelazhagar	13th c. CE	Authoritative synthesis	Vedantic-ethical integration

Chapter 2: Thiruvalluvar — The Man and the Mystery

The Problem of Historical Evidence

Studying Thiruvalluvar through primary sources is deeply challenging. No contemporary biography exists. No clear epigraphic evidence of Thiruvalluvar survives. No documentation of birth, education, profession, or death remains. What is popularly believed about Thiruvalluvar largely comes from traditions formed centuries after the text, which carry cultural significance but cannot be verified as historical fact.

When Did Thiruvalluvar Live?

Evidence Type	Finding	Implication
Linguistic Analysis	Language belongs to early Sangam period	Pre-dates 300 CE with high confidence
Literary Evidence	Later Tamil works cite Kural extensively	Text was well-established by 5th c. CE
Scholarly Consensus	Most scholars: 1st c. BCE to 2nd c. CE	Sangam period peak culture
Keeladi Excavations	Urban Tamil life confirmed 6th c. BCE	Rich cultural context established early
Historical Context	Rome-Tamil trade routes documented	International intellectual environment

Chapter 3: Ancient Tamil Society Behind Thirukkural

Geography and the Five Tinai

Ancient Tamilakam occupied the southern tip of the Indian subcontinent, surrounded by the Arabian Sea to the west, the Bay of Bengal to the east, and the Indian Ocean to the south. The Sangam literary tradition describes five tinai (ecological zones) — kurinji (mountain), mullai (forest), marutam (agricultural plain), neytal (coastal), and palai (arid) — each associated with distinct occupations, social customs, and literary themes.

குறள் 1033 | Kural 1033

உழுதுண்டு வாழ்வாரே வாழ்வார் மற்றெல்லாம் தொழுதுண்டு பின்செல் பவர்.

Uzhudundu vaazhaare vaazhar matreellam thozhudundu pinsel pavar.

Translation: *Those who live by farming truly live; all others follow behind them, bowing to receive food.*

Commentary: This kural reflects the economic reality of ancient Tamilakam. Keeladi archaeological research has revealed burned traces of rice, millet, and legumes, confirming that agriculture was the civilizational backbone. Parimelazhagar: Agriculture is not merely an occupation — it is the foundation upon which all other human activity rests. Modern parallel: The UN Food and Agriculture Organization similarly identifies food security as the precondition for all Sustainable Development Goals.

Trade, Urbanization, and International Connection

Ancient Tamilakam was a key hub in the Indian Ocean trade network, with documented connections to Rome, Egypt, Arabia, Sri Lanka, and Southeast Asia. Archaeological sites including Keeladi, Arikamedu, Korkai, and Alagankulam provide evidence of urban life and international trade that created the cosmopolitan intellectual environment in which Thiruvalluvar flourished.

பகுதி 2 — PART II

நூலை புரிந்துகொள்வோம்

Understanding the Text

Chapter 4: The Architecture of 133 Chapters

Mathematical Perfection as Philosophical Statement

No work in world literature demonstrates as organized a literary architecture as Thirukkural. 133 chapters, each containing exactly 10 kurals. 1,330 kurals total. This mathematical elegance is aligned with a clear philosophical purpose: the number 133 is prime, indivisible, whole — suggesting Thiruvalluvar saw human life as an integrated, undivided unity.

Division	Tamil Name	Chapters	Kurals	Core Concern
Book 1	அறம் (Aram)	1–38	1–380	Virtue, ethics, personal conduct
Book 2	பொருள் (Porul)	39–108	381–1080	Society, governance, economics
Book 3	இன்பம் (Inbam)	109–133	1081–1330	Love, human connection, joy
Total	—	133	1,330	Complete philosophy of human life

This sequence — Aram → Porul → Inbam — carries deep philosophical meaning. Thiruvalluvar does not end his work with governance or religion. He ends up with love. This tells us: a good life is built on ethics, fulfilled in social responsibility, and completed in the deepest human connection.

Chapter 5: The Language of Thirukkural

Key Tamil Ethical Vocabulary

Tamil Word	Transliteration	English Equivalent	Full Semantic Range
அறம்	Aram	Virtue/Duty	righteousness, morality, justice, ethical life
பொருள்	Porul	Material/Governance	wealth, statecraft, social order
இன்பம்	Inbam	Love/Joy	pleasure, happiness, emotional fulfillment
அருள்	Arul	Compassion/Grace	divine grace, human kindness, benevolence
அன்பு	Anbu	Affection/Love	love, family and social bonds
ஒழுக்கம்	Ozhukkam	Conduct/Discipline	ethical behavior, personal discipline
வாய்மை	Vaymai	Truthfulness	language honesty, speaking truth
அடக்கம்	Adakkam	Self-Control	restraint, emotional regulation
அறிவு	Arivu	Wisdom	knowledge, understanding, practical wisdom

Chapter 6: The Great Commentators

Why Commentators Matter

Thirukkural has been preserved across centuries through its commentators. Each generation brought new questions to the text, and the commentaries guided understanding. Without them, the compressed language of the kurals — seven words carrying entire philosophical systems — would be inaccessible.

Commentator	Period	Style	Kural 131 Interpretation
Manakkudavar	9th–10th c.	Clear, contextual	Good conduct is the source of honor; preserved above all possessions.
Parithiyar	10th–11th c.	Practical moral	Ethical conduct determines the value of human life; without it, life's purpose is lost.
Kalingar	11th–12th c.	Linguistics, philosophical	Discipline is the foundation on which other virtues depend; protecting it safeguards ethical order.
Parimelazhagar	13th c.	Authoritative synthesis	Conduct is the highest expression of virtue; must be preserved even at personal cost.

பகுதி 3 — PART III

அறம் — ARAM: Virtue and Ethics

Having established the foundations of ethics, truth, and compassion in the opening chapters, Thiruvalluvar now constructs the complete edifice of personal virtue. These thirteen chapters move outward in concentric circles — from the mastery of one's own self, through the bonds of friendship and family, to the social virtues of generosity and reputation, and finally to the disciplines of restraint that protect virtue from its most common enemies: greed, envy, slander, idle speech, and anger. Read in sequence, they form a single argument: that a flourishing outer life is impossible without a governed inner one.

Chapter 7: The Foundation of Ethics

Mental Purity — The Essence of Virtue

Thiruvalluvar begins not with governance, economics, or social organization — but with virtue. Because all human achievement ultimately rests on an ethical foundation. A civilization built on corrupt inner life will eventually collapse regardless of its material wealth or military power.

குறள் 34 | Kural 34

மனத்துக்கண் மாசிலன் ஆதல் அனைத்தறன் ஆகுல நீர பிற.

Manathukkan maasilaan aadhal anaintaran aagula neer pira.

Translation: *Mental purity is the foundation of all virtue; all else is of no account compared to this.*

Commentary: Parimelazhagar: Virtue manifests in action but originates in mind. Even if one appears virtuous outwardly, if the mind is corrupted by envy, greed, or deceit, true virtue is absent. Manakkudavar: The mind is the source from which all ethical conduct springs. Kalingar: External acts of virtue are merely the visible surface; the invisible foundation is mental purity. Modern Psychology (Jonathan Haidt): Moral cognition research confirms that ethical action originates from internal mental frameworks and emotional dispositions, not merely social rules.

Comparative Philosophy: Mental Purity Across Traditions

Aristotle

Concept: Virtue emerges from character (ethos), not mere rule-following

Parallel Kural: Kural 34 — Inner purity precedes outer virtue

Both Aristotle and Thiruvalluvar agree: virtue is a state of character, not a list of rules. The Nicomachean Ethics (Book II) argues that virtuous acts must come from a virtuous character — precisely what Kural 34 expresses in seven words.

Buddha

Concept: Purity of mind precedes all action — "Mind is the forerunner of all actions" (Dhammapada 1)

Parallel Kural: Kural 34 — Mental impurity corrupts all outward virtue

The parallel is striking. Both the Dhammapada and Kural 34 place mental purity as the absolute prerequisite of ethical life. The difference: Buddhism emphasizes liberation from attachment; Thiruvalluvar emphasizes active engagement in ethical social life.

Kant

Concept: Good will is the only unconditionally good thing — acts have moral worth only if motivated by duty

Parallel Kural: Kural 34 — Purity of intention determines true virtue

Kant's "good will" in the Groundwork of the Metaphysics of Morals (1785) maps onto Thiruvalluvar's "mental purity" (manas-suddhi). Both argue that the moral quality of an act is determined by inner intention, not outer consequence.

குறள் 38 | Kural 38

திறனல்ல தீய பிறர்க்கு நேராமை தீர்த்தம் ஆகும்.

Thiranal theeya pirarkku neraami theertham aagum.

Translation: *Avoiding actions that harm others, even when one has the power to harm, is the highest purification.*

Commentary: Parithiyar: Power unused for harm is the ultimate ethical test. Kalingar: Having capacity for harm and restraining it demonstrates mastery of the self — a higher virtue than simple incapacity. Modern parallel: Hannah Arendt's concept of political responsibility — the true measure of character is what we refrain from doing when we could act with impunity. AI Ethics application: The capacity to surveil, manipulate, or harm does not create the right to do so.

Modern Applications: Mental Purity in the 21st Century

Domain	Thiruvalluvar's Principle	Contemporary Application
Leadership Ethics	Mental purity precedes ethical leadership	Leaders who cultivate inner integrity create ethical organizational cultures
Corporate Governance	True virtue cannot be performative	ESG initiatives must reflect genuine values, not greenwashing
AI Alignment	Internal values determine external behavior	AI systems need value alignment, not just behavioral constraints
Medical Ethics	Intent determines the moral quality of action	Informed consent requires transparency of intent, not just information transfer
Legal Systems	Mental state (mens rea) determines guilt	Criminal law's concept of intent directly parallels Kural 34's insight

Chapter 8: Truth and Integrity — வாய்மை

Truth (vaymai) in Thirukkural is not merely the absence of lying. It is a positive force — the alignment of inner knowing with outward expression. Thiruvalluvar argues that truth-telling is not just morally required; it is the foundation of all human relationships and social trust.

குறள் 291 | Kural 291

தன்னெஞ்சு அறிவது பொய்யற்க, பொய்த்தபின் தன்னெஞ்சே தன்னைச் சுடும்.

Thannenchu arividhu poyyarka, poitthapin thannence thannai sudum.

Translation: *Speak not what your own heart knows to be false; for after speaking falsely, your own heart will burn you.*

Commentary: Parimelazhagar: The ultimate court of truth is not external — it is the conscience. Lying corrupts the speaker more than the listener. Manakkudavar: Truth-speaking is not primarily about others — it is the self-respecting life. Kalingar: The heart knows truth; violating that knowledge creates inner disintegration. Modern Psychology: Research in moral disengagement (Bandura) confirms that self-justification of dishonesty gradually erodes moral agency. Legal parallel: Perjury laws recognize that false testimony corrupts not just the court but the witness.

குறள் 294 | Kural 294

மனத்தொடு வாய்மை மொழியின் தவத்தொடு தான் தவம் செய்வான் எவன்?

Manadodu vaymai mozhiyin thavadodu thaan thavam seyvan evan?

Translation: *If one speaks truth aligned with the heart, what need is there for ascetic practices?*

Commentary: This is Thiruvalluvar at his most direct. Truth-speaking, when it comes from genuine inner alignment, is itself the highest spiritual discipline. This challenges the idea that spiritual virtue requires withdrawal from ordinary life — the honest merchant, the truthful official, the transparent leader are themselves practicing the highest form of ethics. Comparable to Gandhi's satyagraha: truth-force as the foundation of social and political transformation.

Chapter 9: Compassion and Nonviolence — அருள்

Arul (compassion/grace) is one of the central pillars of Thirukkural's ethical system. Unlike systems that treat compassion as a supplementary virtue, Thiruvalluvar places it at the foundation — the capacity to feel and respond to the suffering of all living beings is what makes human ethics possible.

குறள் 241 | Kural 241

அருட்செல்வம் செல்வத்துள் செல்வம் பொருட்செல்வம் பூரியார் கண்ணும் உள.

Arut selam selvathul selvam, porul selvam pooriyar kannum ula.

Translation: *The wealth of compassion is the greatest of all wealth; material wealth can be found even among the wicked.*

Commentary: Parimelazhagar: Material wealth is ethically neutral — the wicked have it as much as the virtuous. Only compassion as wealth confers genuine human dignity. Parithiyar: Compassion is the only wealth that grows through giving. Kalingar: Arul is the defining quality of the fully realized human being. Comparative: In Buddhist terms, karuna (compassion) is the highest form of dana (giving). In Stoicism, sympatheia — the felt connection with all humanity — is the cosmopolitan virtue that unites the rational community of humans.

குறள் 321 | Kural 321

கொல்லாமை மேற்கொள் வேண்டும்.

Kollamai merkkol ventum.

Translation: *One must adopt nonviolence as the supreme principle of life.*

Commentary: This is one of Thirukkural's most uncompromising positions. Nonviolence (kollamai) is not presented as an ideal to aspire to — it is presented as a foundational commitment. Parimelazhagar: All other virtues flow from the refusal to harm. Manakkudavar: The measure of a civilization is how it treats the most vulnerable. Parallels: Ahimsa in Jainism and early Buddhism; Gandhi's satyagraha; the United Nations Universal Declaration of Human Rights Article 3 (right to life and security); Peter Singer's utilitarian animal ethics.

Chapter 10 Self-Control and Character — அடக்கமுடைமை

If there is a single virtue Thiruvalluvar treats as the gatekeeper of all others, it is self-discipline (adakkam). Before one can be generous, truthful, just, or loving, one must first be able to govern oneself. Self-mastery, in the Kural's vision, is not repression but elevation — the disciplined self rises toward the company of the gods, while the ungoverned self falls into darkness. The chapter's most enduring contribution is its insistence that the hardest power to hold is power over oneself.

குறள் 121 | Kural 121

அடக்கம் அமரருள் உய்க்கும் அடங்காமை ஆரிருள் உய்த்து விடும்.

Adakkam amararul uykkum; adangaamai aariruL uyttu vidum.

Translation: *Self-control lifts one to the company of the gods; the want of it casts one into deepest darkness.*

Commentary: Parimelazhagar: Adakkam is the disciplined ordering of speech, action, and desire — the ladder by which the soul ascends. Manakkudavar: The contrast is deliberate — light and darkness, ascent and fall — marking self-control as the decisive fork of the moral life. Kalingar: "Darkness" here is not punishment imposed from outside but the natural consequence of a life that has lost its rudder. Modern parallel: Research on self-regulation (Walter Mischel's "marshmallow" studies; Roy Baumeister's work on willpower) confirms that the capacity to delay gratification predicts life outcomes more reliably than almost any other single trait.

குறள் 127 | Kural 127

யாகாவா ராயினும் நாகாக்க காவாக்காற் சோகாப்பர் சொல்லிழுக்குப் பட்டு.

Yaakaavaa raayinum naakaakka; kaavaakkaal sokaappar sollizhukkup pattu.

Translation: *Whatever else you fail to guard, guard the tongue; for the unguarded tongue brings grief through its own slips.*

Commentary: Parithiyar: Of all the faculties to discipline, speech is the most urgent, for its errors cannot be recalled. Parimelazhagar: The tongue is singled out because its lapses are instantaneous and irreversible — a guarded mind can still be undone by an unguarded word. Modern application: In an age of instant publication, where a single message can circle the globe before it can be retracted, this kural reads as a direct ethics of digital speech.

Comparative Philosophy

Aristotle	Sophrosyne (temperance) — the disciplined mean between excess and deficiency of desire.
Parallel	*Kural 121 — self-control as the elevating virtue.*
Synthesis	Both treat self-mastery not as the denial of desire but as its rational governance. For Aristotle the temperate person desires the right things in the right measure; for Thiruvalluvar adakkam is the trained capacity that makes every other virtue possible.

Stoicism	Enkrateia — command over the passions as the precondition of freedom.
Parallel	*Kural 127 — guarding speech and impulse.*
Synthesis	The Stoic distinction between what is "up to us" and what is not maps closely onto the Kural's focus: we cannot govern fortune, but we can govern the tongue, the temper, and the will. Self-discipline is, for both, the only durable form of liberty.

Self-Discipline in the 21st Century

Domain	Principle of Adakkam	Contemporary Application
Digital Life	Guard the tongue	Pausing before posting; resisting reactive, viral outrage
Leadership	Power over self precedes power over others	Emotional regulation as a core executive competency
Health	Mastery of impulse	Behavioral models of habit formation and addiction recovery
Finance	Delay of gratification	Long-horizon saving over impulsive consumption

Chapter 11 Friendship and Human Relationships—நட்பு

Few subjects receive warmer or more searching treatment in the Kural than friendship (natpu). Thiruvalluvar regards true friendship as among the hardest things to attain and the surest protection against misfortune. Crucially, he distinguishes friendship from mere companionship: the genuine friend is the one who restrains us from wrong and rushes to our aid in distress, not the one who merely shares our pleasures. Friendship, for the Kural, is a moral relationship before it is a social one.

குறள் 781 | Kural 781

செயற்கரிய யாவுள நட்பின் அதுபோல் வினைக்கரிய யாவுள காப்பு.

Seyarkariya yaavula natpin; adhupol vinaikkariya yaavula kaappu.

Translation: *What is harder to acquire than friendship? And what surer protection against every trial?*

Commentary: Parimelazhagar: True friendship is rare precisely because it cannot be manufactured — it must be discerned, tested, and earned over time. Manakkudavar: The kural pairs difficulty with value — the hard-won friendship is also the strongest shield. Kalingar: "Protection" here is moral as much as practical: the true friend guards us from our own errors.

குறள் 788 | Kural 788

உடுக்கை இழந்தவன் கைபோல ஆங்கே இடுக்கண் களைவதாம் நட்பு.

Udukkai izhanthavan kaipola aange; idukkan kalaivadhaam natpu.

Translation: *As the hand instantly catches the slipping garment, true friendship removes distress the very moment it appears.*

Commentary: This is among the most celebrated images in all of Tamil literature. Parithiyar: The hand does not deliberate before saving the garment — it acts by reflex, from love, without being asked. Parimelazhagar: True friendship is this reflex of care — unhesitating, unbidden, and instant. Modern Psychology: Studies of social support identify "responsiveness" — immediate, attuned aid in distress — as the strongest predictor of relationship durability.

Comparative Philosophy

Aristotle	**Philia of virtue — the highest friendship is between good people who wish each other's good for its own sake.**
Parallel	*Kural 781, 788 — friendship as moral bond and reflexive aid.*
Synthesis	Aristotle's three friendships — of utility, pleasure, and virtue — culminate in the last, which alone endures. Thiruvalluvar reaches the same summit: the friend who removes distress without being asked is the friend of virtue, valued not for use or pleasure but for the good itself.

Friendship in the 21st Century

In an era of "networks" and "connections" measured in the thousands, the Kural's austere standard is clarifying: a contact list is not a circle of friends. The test of friendship is not visibility in good times but presence in distress — the hand that catches the falling garment. Research on loneliness in connected societies confirms what Thiruvalluvar implies: the quantity of contacts has risen while the quality of friendship, by his measure, has not.

Chapter 12 Family and Domestic Life — இல்வாழ்க்கை

Against ascetic traditions that locate the highest life in withdrawal from the world, Thiruvalluvar makes a radical claim: the householder who lives rightly is the equal — indeed the support — of the renunciant. The home (illvazhkkai) is not a lower station to be escaped but the central training ground of virtue, where compassion, hospitality, truthfulness, and self-restraint are practiced daily upon those nearest to us. The well-lived domestic life sustains the ascetic, the ancestor, the guest, the kindred, and the self alike.

குறள் 41 | Kural 41

இல்வாழ்வான் என்பான் இயல்புடைய மூவர்க்கும் நல்லாற்றின் நின்ற துணை.

Ilvaazhvaan enbaan iyalpudaiya moovarkkum; nallaatrin ninra thunai.

Translation: *The true householder is a steadfast support, on the path of virtue, to all three who strive — the student, the ascetic, and the ancestor.*

Commentary: Parimelazhagar: The household is not a retreat from duty but the hub that supports every other way of life. Manakkudavar: The householder sustains the celibate student, the renunciant, and honors the departed — the home is the load-bearing pillar of society. Kalingar: Domestic virtue is the most demanding discipline precisely because it is unglamorous and unending.

குறள் 47 | Kural 47

இயல்பினான் இல்வாழ்க்கை வாழ்பவன் என்பான் முயல்வாருள் எல்லாம் தலை.

Iyalpinaan ilvaazhkkai vaazhpavan enbaan; muyalvaarul ellaam thalai.

Translation: *One who lives the household life by right principle stands foremost among all who strive for the good.*

Commentary: Parithiyar: The householder who fulfils duty without abandoning the world achieves more than the one who flees it. Parimelazhagar: "Foremost among all who strive" is a deliberate elevation — the moral athlete of ordinary life ranks above the spectacular renunciant. Modern parallel: Contemporary ethics of care (Carol Gilligan; Nel Noddings) similarly relocate the moral center of gravity from abstract principle to the concrete relationships of daily life.

Comparative Philosophy

Confucius	**The cultivated home as the root of the ordered state — “self, family, state, world.”**
Parallel	*Kural 41, 47 — the household as the foundation of social virtue.*
Synthesis	For Confucius, social order radiates outward from the rightly governed family; filial and domestic virtue is the seed of public order. Thiruvalluvar shares this architecture exactly: the home is where the virtues that later govern the polity are first learned and practiced.

Domestic Life in the 21st Century

- Work-life integration: the Kural’s elevation of domestic duty challenges a culture that treats career as the only arena of achievement.
- Care economy: it anticipates the modern recognition that unpaid domestic and caregiving labor is the invisible foundation of all public life.
- Hospitality and community: the household as a place of welcome counters the privatization and isolation of contemporary home life.

Chapter 13 The Fear of Evil Deeds — தீவினையச்சம்

Thiruvalluvar draws a sharp line between two kinds of restraint: the fear of being caught and the fear of doing wrong. The truly virtuous person fears the evil act itself — not its external consequences. This interiorization of moral fear is one of the Kural's most psychologically sophisticated moves: it locates the deterrent to wrongdoing inside the conscience rather than in the threat of punishment, producing a person who behaves well even when no one is watching.

குறள் 201 | Kural 201

தீவினையார் அஞ்சார் விழுமியார் அஞ்சுவர் தீவினை என்னும் செருக்கு.
Theevinaiyaar anjaar vizhumiyaar anjuvar; theevinai ennum serukku.

Translation: *The wicked do not fear evil deeds; the noble dread even the arrogance that makes evil seem permissible.*

Commentary: Parimelazhagar: The noble fear not punishment but the inner corruption that wrongdoing produces. Kalingar: "Arrogance" (serukku) is the precise psychological root — evil begins in the conceit that one is above the moral order. Modern Psychology: This anticipates the distinction between an "external" conscience (fear of consequences) and an "internal" one (fear of self-betrayal), the latter being the mark of mature moral development (Kohlberg).

குறள் 205 | Kural 205

இலன் என்று தீயவை செய்யற்க செய்யின் இலனாகும் மற்றும் பெயர்த்து.
Ilan enru theeyavai seyyarka; seyyin ilanaagum matrum peyarttu.

Translation: *Do not do evil pleading poverty; such deeds will only make you poorer than before.*

Commentary: Parimelazhagar: Wrongdoing chosen as a shortcut out of hardship deepens the very hardship it sought to escape. Parithiyar: Poverty is no licence for harm — the moral law does not suspend itself for the desperate. Modern parallel: Behavioral economics confirms that desperation-driven unethical shortcuts (fraud, theft) statistically worsen long-run outcomes for the perpetrator — the kural's warning is empirically borne out.

Comparative Philosophy

Kant	The good will acts from duty, not from fear of consequence — moral worth lies in the motive.
Parallel	*Kural 201 — dreading the wrong act itself, not its punishment.*
Synthesis	Kant's central insight — that an act has moral worth only when done because it is right, not because it is rewarded or safe — is precisely the Kural's distinction. Both relocate morality from the calculus of consequence to the integrity of the inner motive.

Fear of Wrong in the 21st Century

Modern governance distinguishes between compliance (avoiding penalties) and integrity (doing right for its own sake). Organizations built only on surveillance and sanction produce people who calculate the odds of being caught; organizations built on internalized values produce people who do not need to be watched. Thiruvalluvar identified this distinction two thousand years before it became the central question of corporate ethics and institutional design.

Chapter 14 Knowing What Is Fitting — ஒப்புரவு அறிதல்

Oppuravu is one of the Kural's most subtle ethical concepts: the art of acting fittingly — reading the situation accurately and giving each circumstance its due. It is closely linked to disinterested benevolence: the wise person does good as the rain-cloud does, expecting nothing in return. Right action, in this vision, is not the mechanical application of rules but a trained sensitivity to context, proportion, and the genuine needs of the moment.

குறள் 211 | Kural 211

கைம்மாறு வேண்டா கடப்பாடு மாரிமாட்டு என் ஆற்றுங் கொல்லோ உலகு.

Kaimmaaru venda kadappaadu; maarimaattu en aatrung kollo ulagu.

Translation: *True benevolence looks for no return — what repayment does the world give back to the rain-cloud?*

Commentary: Parimelazhagar: The rain-cloud is the perfect image of disinterested giving — it pours without contract or expectation. Manakkudavar: Duty done for reward is trade, not benevolence; oppuravu is giving released from the logic of exchange. Kalingar: The world receives the rain and offers nothing back — yet the cloud returns each season. So acts the truly generous person.

குறள் 212 | Kural 212

தாளாற்றித் தந்த பொருளெல்லாம் தக்கார்க்கு வேளாண்மை செய்தற் பொருட்டு.

Thaalaatrith thantha porulellaam thakkaarkku; velaanmai seydhar poruttu.

Translation: *All wealth gathered through honest effort is meant for the doing of good to those who are worthy.*

Commentary: Parithiyar: Wealth is justified not by its accumulation but by the good it enables. Parimelazhagar: Effort and ethics together — wealth honestly earned, then rightly spent — complete the circle of oppuravu. Modern parallel: The ethic of "stewardship" in philanthropy and the concept of wealth as a social trust both restate this kural's claim that earning is incomplete without fitting giving.

Knowing What Is Fitting in the 21st Century

Domain	Oppuravu Principle	Application
Philanthropy	Give without expecting return	Effective altruism; unconditional aid
Professional ethics	Read the context, act in proportion	Situational judgment over rigid rule-following
Public policy	Wealth as social trust	Progressive responsibility of the prosperous

Chapter 15 Generosity — ஈகை

If oppuravu is fitting benevolence, eekai is its purest form: the act of giving to those who can give nothing back. Thiruvalluvar is precise — only giving to the needy is true charity; everything else, given in expectation of return, is a transaction wearing the mask of generosity. The relief of hunger, in particular, is singled out as the highest use to which wealth can be put: there is no securer treasury than the gratitude of the poor whose suffering one has relieved.

குறள் 221 | Kural 221

வறியார்க்கொன்று ஈவதே ஈகை மற்றெல்லாம் குறியெதிர்ப்பை நீர துடைத்து.

Variyaarkkonru eevadhe eekai; matrellaam kuriyedhirppai neera udaittu.

Translation: *To give to the destitute alone is true charity; all other giving expects something in return.*

Commentary: Parimelazhagar: The defining mark of eekai is the inability of the receiver to repay — only then is the gift pure. Manakkudavar: Gifts to the rich or powerful are investments; gifts to the poor are virtue. Kalingar: The kural strips charity of its self-interested counterfeits.

குறள் 226 | Kural 226

அற்றார் அழிபசி தீர்த்தல் அஃதொருவன் பெற்றான் பொருள்வைப் புழி.

Atraar azhipasi theerttal; ahdhoruvan petraan porulvaip puzhi.

Translation: *To relieve the killing hunger of the destitute — that is the safest vault in which one can store one's wealth.*

Commentary: Parithiyar: Wealth spent on relieving hunger is not lost but invested in the most secure of all treasuries. Parimelazhagar: "Killing hunger" underscores urgency — the relief of acute need is the noblest expenditure. Modern parallel: The UN's designation of "Zero Hunger" as a foundational Sustainable Development Goal restates Thiruvalluvar's ranking of priorities — the relief of hunger is the precondition of every other good.

Comparative Philosophy

Buddhism	**Dana (selfless giving) — the first of the perfections, purest when given without attachment to merit.**
Parallel	*Kural 221 — charity defined by the giver's freedom from expectation of return.*
Synthesis	Both traditions distinguish giving-as-trade from giving-as-virtue. The Buddhist ideal of dana given without clinging to its reward is exactly the Kural's standard: the gift is pure only when the giver expects nothing back.

Generosity in the 21st Century

The Kural's test — does the receiver have power to repay? — cuts cleanly through modern "strategic philanthropy" that gives to the visible and the influential. Genuine generosity, by this measure, is directed toward those who cannot reciprocate: the hungry, the displaced, the forgotten. It is a standard that indicts charity-as-marketing and elevates the quiet, unrewarded gift.

Chapter 16 Fame and Reputation — புகழ்

For Thiruvalluvar, the only form of immortality available to mortals is the lasting memory of virtuous deeds. Fame (pugazh) is not vanity or celebrity — it is the moral afterlife of a well-lived life, the imperishable trace that good action leaves in the world. To be born and leave no such trace is, in the Kural's stark formulation, hardly to have been born at all. Reputation here is inseparable from virtue: enduring fame can only be built on real goodness.

குறள் 231 | Kural 231

ஈதல் இசைபட வாழ்தல் அதுவல்லது ஊதியம் இல்லை உயிர்க்கு.

Eedhal isaipada vaazhdhal; adhuvalladhu oodhiyam illai uyirkku.

Translation: *To give, and to live so that good is spoken of you — there is no greater gain for any soul than this.*

Commentary: Parimelazhagar: Giving and the honor it earns are the only true profit of a human life. Manakkudavar: "Gain" is redefined — not wealth accumulated but goodness remembered. Kalingar: The two are linked — lasting fame grows from genuine giving, never from display alone.

குறள் 236 | Kural 236

தோன்றின் புகழொடு தோன்றுக அஃதிலார் தோன்றலின் தோன்றாமை நன்று.

Thondrin pugazhodu thondruga; ahdhilaar thondralin thondraamai nandru.

Translation: *If you are to come into being, come with fame; for those who cannot, it is better not to have been born at all.*

Commentary: Parithiyar: A life that leaves no honorable trace has missed its purpose. Parimelazhagar: The kural is intentionally severe — to live without earning lasting good repute is to waste the gift of existence. Modern reading: Stripped of its rhetoric, the kural asks the question every reflective person eventually faces — what will remain of me that was worth the living?

Comparative Philosophy

Stoicism / Aristotle	**The good life leaves a lasting legacy of virtuous action; honor follows virtue rather than being pursued for itself.**
Parallel	*Kural 231, 236 — fame as the moral residue of goodness, not its goal.*
Synthesis	Aristotle warns against pursuing honor for its own sake — true honor tracks virtue. Thiruvalluvar agrees: pugazh worth having cannot be manufactured by self-promotion; it is the shadow that real goodness casts across time.

Reputation in the 21st Century

The age of personal branding and viral celebrity inverts the Kural's teaching: it offers fame detached from virtue, visibility without substance. Thiruvalluvar's standard restores the link — the only reputation worth building is one founded on real good done for others. A name that survives because of genuine contribution is the kural's pugazh; a name that trends and is forgotten is its counterfeit.

Chapter 17 Not Coveting What Belongs to Others — பிறனில் விழையாமை

Thiruvalluvar treats the desire for what is another's — most pointedly, another's spouse — as a corruption that poisons the one who harbors it long before it harms anyone else. Coveting is presented not merely as a social offense but as a self-inflicted wound: it brings enmity, sin, fear, and disgrace, four shadows that never leave the one who transgresses. The chapter is a study in how desire misdirected destroys the desirer.

குறள் 141 | Kural 141

பிறன்பொருளாள் பெட்டொழுகும் பேதைமை ஞாலத்து அறம்பொருள் கண்டார்கண் இல்.

Piranporulaal pettozhugum pedhaimai; gnaalattu aramporul kandaarkan il.

Translation: *The folly of desiring another's wife is never found in those who have understood virtue and the true nature of wealth.*

Commentary: Parimelazhagar: Those who grasp what virtue and wealth really are cannot stoop to coveting — the very understanding immunizes them. Manakkudavar: "Folly" (pedhaimai) is the operative word — coveting is portrayed as stupidity, not merely sin. Kalingar: The desire for the forbidden reveals a failure to comprehend one's own good.

குறள் 146 | Kural 146

பகைபாவம் அச்சம் பழியென நான்கும் இகவாவாம் இல்லிறப்பான் கண்.

Pagaipaavam achcham pazhiyena naangum; igavaavaam illirappaan kan.

Translation: *Enmity, sin, fear, and disgrace — these four never depart from the one who violates another's home.*

Commentary: Parithiyar: The four consequences are inescapable — they shadow the transgressor permanently. Parimelazhagar: The kural enumerates with legal precision the full cost of the act — social, moral, psychological, and reputational. Modern Psychology: Research on guilt, anxiety, and social exclusion confirms the cluster — betrayal of trust reliably produces enmity, chronic fear of exposure, and lasting reputational damage.

Comparative Philosophy

Kant	**Treating persons as ends, never merely as means — covetous use of another violates their dignity.**
Parallel	*Kural 141, 146 — coveting as a corruption that degrades both desirer and desired.*
Synthesis	Kant's prohibition on using others as mere instruments of one's desire underlies the Kural's warning. To covet what belongs to another is to reduce persons and relationships to objects of appetite — a violation of dignity that, the Kural insists, rebounds upon the violator.

Non-Coveting in the 21st Century

Beyond its literal subject, the chapter's deeper teaching concerns the discipline of desire in a culture engineered to inflame it. Advertising, social media, and status competition are designed to make us want what is another's. The Kural's insight — that misdirected desire corrodes the desirer first — is a direct counter to the architecture of modern envy.

Chapter 18 Patience and Forbearance — பொறையுடைமை

Poraiyudaimai — the strength to endure wrong without retaliating — is one of the Kural's great paradoxes: it presents restraint not as weakness but as the highest power. The image is unforgettable: just as the earth bears even those who dig into it, the truly strong bear those who injure them. To forgive a wrong is good; to forget it entirely is better still. Forbearance, in this vision, is the quiet sovereignty of the self-possessed over the reactive.

குறள் 151 | Kural 151

அகழ்வாரைத் தாங்கும் நிலம்போலத் தம்மை இகழ்வார்ப் பொறுத்தல் தலை.

Agazhvaarai thaangum nilampola thammai; igazhvaarp poruttal thalai.

Translation: *As the earth bears even those who dig into it, to bear with those who scorn us is the highest virtue.*

Commentary: Parimelazhagar: The earth-image is exact — it sustains the very ones who wound it, without complaint or retaliation. Manakkudavar: Forbearance is ranked "the highest" (thalai) precisely because it is the hardest. Kalingar: The patient person, like the earth, draws strength from steadiness rather than from striking back.

குறள் 152 | Kural 152

பொறுத்தல் இறப்பினை என்றும் அதனை மறத்தல் அதனினும் நன்று.

Poruttal irappinai endrum; adhanai marattal adhaninum nandru.

Translation: *To forbear the wrongs of others is always good; but to forget them entirely is better still.*

Commentary: Parithiyar: Patience that still remembers the wrong is incomplete — true forbearance releases the memory as well. Parimelazhagar: Forgetting here is not weakness of mind but freedom from resentment. Modern Psychology: Research on forgiveness (Everett Worthington; the REACH model) confirms that releasing the grievance — not merely suppressing the urge to retaliate — is what restores psychological wellbeing.

Comparative Philosophy

Stoicism	**The wise person is unmoved by insult — injury depends on our judgment of it, not on the act itself.**
Parallel	*Kural 151, 152 — bearing and then releasing the wrong.*
Synthesis	Marcus Aurelius counsels meeting offense with equanimity, recognizing that the power to wound us lies in our own reaction. Thiruvalluvar reaches further: not only endure the insult but forget it, freeing the self entirely from the grip of grievance.

Forbearance in the 21st Century

In a culture of instant retaliation — the reply, the call-out, the escalating feud — the Kural's elevation of patience is countercultural. It reframes the refusal to retaliate not as defeat but as mastery. Conflict-resolution research, restorative justice, and the psychology of forgiveness all converge on Thiruvalluvar's ancient claim: the one who can absorb a wrong without returning it holds the real power.

Chapter 19 Freedom from Envy — அழுக்காறாமை

Envy (azhukkaru) receives some of the Kural's most penetrating psychological analysis. Thiruvalluvar's central claim is counterintuitive and profound: envy harms its possessor before it touches its object. The envious person, resenting another's good fortune, forfeits both virtue and prosperity for themselves. No one has ever risen by envy, and no one free of it has ever fallen. Freedom from envy is thus not merely a moral nicety but a precondition of one's own flourishing.

குறள் 163 | Kural 163

அறன்ஆக்கம் வேண்டாதான் என்பான் பிறனாக்கம் பேணாது அழுக்கறுப் பான்.

Aran-aakkam vendaadhaan enbaan; piranaakkam penaadhu azhukkaruppaan.

Translation: *The one who envies another's prosperity, unable to bear it, in effect wants neither virtue nor wealth for himself.*

Commentary: Parimelazhagar: To resent another's good is to reject one's own good — envy is self-defeating at its root. Manakkudavar: The envious forfeit both moral and material gain, sacrificing their own welfare to their resentment. Kalingar: Envy is the one vice whose first and worst victim is always the one who harbors it.

குறள் 170 | Kural 170

அழுக்கற்று அகன்றாரும் இல்லை அஃதில்லார் பெருக்கத்தில் தீர்ந்தாரும் இல்.

Azhukkatru aganraarum illai; ahdhillaar perukkattil theerndhaarum il.

Translation: *None ever rose to greatness through envy; and none free of envy ever fell from prosperity.*

Commentary: Parithiyar: History offers no example of envy producing greatness — the ledger is empty on one side and full on the other. Parimelazhagar: The kural states an empirical law of the moral life. Modern Psychology: Studies of "malicious" versus "benign" envy confirm that resentful envy correlates with diminished wellbeing and performance, while admiration directed toward emulation correlates with growth.

Freedom from Envy in the 21st Century

Social media has been described as an envy-generation machine — a constant stream of others' curated successes designed to provoke comparison. The Kural's diagnosis is precise and ancient: comparison-driven resentment impoverishes the one who feels it. Its prescription is equally clear — freedom from envy is not generosity toward others so much as a gift one gives oneself.

Chapter 20 Avoiding Slander and Backbittingt — புறங்கூறாமை

Thiruvalluvar reserves particular contempt for slander — speaking ill of someone behind their back. The offense is twofold: it violates truth, and it violates the dignity of a person who cannot answer. Strikingly, the Kural argues that even harsh criticism spoken to a person's face is preferable to soft words spoken in their absence, because the former at least respects the person enough to confront them directly. The slanderer, moreover, exposes their own faults in the very act of exposing another's.

குறள் 184 | Kural 184

கண்ணின்று கண்அறச் சொல்லினும் சொல்லற்க முன்னின்று பின்நோக்காச் சொல்.

Kanninru kanarach chollinum sollarka; munninru pinnokkaach chol.

Translation: *Even harsh words spoken to a person's face are better than gentle words spoken behind their back, where they cannot reply.*

Commentary: Parimelazhagar: To speak ill of the absent is cowardice dressed as conversation — the absent cannot defend themselves. Manakkudavar: Direct criticism, however blunt, respects the person; covert slander does not. Kalingar: The presence of the criticized makes even hard words honest; their absence makes even soft words a betrayal.

குறள் 186 | Kural 186

பிறன்பழி கூறுவான் தன்பழி யுள்ளும் திறன்தெரிந்து கூறப் படும்.

Piranpazhi kooruvaan thanpazhi yullum; thirandherindhu koorap padum.

Translation: *The one who broadcasts another's faults will find his own faults examined and exposed in turn.*

Commentary: Parithiyar: Slander invites reciprocal scrutiny — the one who points fingers draws eyes to their own conduct. Parimelazhagar: The slanderer's very speech becomes the warrant for investigating the slanderer. Modern parallel: Reputational research confirms that habitual disparagers are themselves perceived as less trustworthy — slander damages the speaker's standing as much as the target's.

Non-Slander in the 21st Century

The digital age has made covert disparagement frictionless: the anonymous comment, the screenshot shared without context, the pile-on directed at someone who is absent and outnumbered. The Kural's standard is a direct rebuke — if a criticism cannot be spoken honestly to the person's face, it should not be spoken behind their back. Honest confrontation, however uncomfortable, respects the dignity that slander destroys.

Chapter 21 Avoiding Vain and Useless Speech — பயனில சொல்லாமை

For Thiruvalluvar, speech is sacred — a faculty whose power must not be squandered on empty words. To speak much and say nothing, to fill the air with talk devoid of worth, is to earn the contempt of all and to waste the most distinctively human gift. The discipline is not silence but significance: speak words that carry value, and refuse to speak words that carry none. Useless speech, the Kural notes, is worse than unkind action toward friends — a striking ranking that measures the seriousness with which it treats words.

குறள் 192 | Kural 192

பயனில பல்லார்முன் சொல்லல் நயனில நட்டார்கண் செய்தலின் தீது.
Payanila pallaarmun sollal; nayanila nattaarkan seydhalin theedhu.

Translation: *To utter worthless words before many is a greater evil than doing unkind acts to one's own friends.*

Commentary: Parimelazhagar: The kural ranks the waste of speech above unkindness to friends in seriousness — a measure of how gravely it treats the misuse of words. Manakkudavar: Empty speech before an assembly squanders the trust of many at once. Kalingar: Words have weight; to scatter them without worth is to debase a sacred currency.

குறள் 200 | Kural 200

சொல்லுக சொல்லில் பயனுடைய சொல்லற்க சொல்லில் பயனிலாச் சொல்.
Solluga sollil payanudaiya; sollarka sollil payanilaach chol.

Translation: *Speak only words that carry worth; never speak words that are empty of all worth.*

Commentary: Parithiyar: The rule is symmetrical and absolute — speak the valuable, refuse the worthless. Parimelazhagar: Significance, not volume, is the measure of good speech. Modern parallel: In an age of information overload, the discipline of "signal over noise" — communicating only what carries genuine value — is precisely this kural's ancient counsel.

Vain Speech in the 21st Century

- Information ecology: the kural's "signal over noise" anticipates the modern challenge of attention amid endless trivial content.
- Meeting culture: it indicts the corporate ritual of talk that conveys nothing — the meeting that should have been a sentence.
- Mindful communication: it aligns with contemporary practices that prize intentional, value-bearing speech over compulsive filling of silence.

Chapter 22 Freedom from Anger — வெகுளாமை

The Kural's treatment of anger is among its most psychologically acute. Anger is portrayed not as righteous force but as a destroyer — it kills the smile and the joy of the face, it consumes its possessor, and what it destroys in seconds may have taken years of virtue to build. Crucially, Thiruvalluvar measures restraint by its effect: to curb anger where it could prevail is true mastery; to curb it where it is powerless is meaningless. The one who renounces anger entirely is ranked with the great renunciants.

குறள் 304 | Kural 304
நகையும் உவகையும் கொல்லும் சினத்தின் பகையும் உளவோ பிறிது. *Nagaiyum uvagaiyum kollum sinattin; pagaiyum ulavo piridhu.*
Translation: *Anger murders the smile and the joy of the face — is there any enemy more destructive than this?*
Commentary: Parimelazhagar: Anger is named the supreme enemy because it destroys the very capacities — joy and warmth — that make life worth living. Manakkudavar: It strikes first at the angry person's own happiness. Kalingar: The smile and joy it kills are one's own — anger is self-inflicted before it is anything else.

குறள் 310 | Kural 310
இறந்தார் இறந்தார் அனையர் சினத்தைத் துறந்தார் துறந்தார் துணை. *Iranthaar iranthaar anaiyar; sinattai thuranthaar thuranthaar thunai.*
Translation: *Those who give way to wrath are as good as dead; those who renounce anger are the equals of the great renunciants.*
Commentary: Parithiyar: To surrender to anger is a kind of death; to renounce it is a kind of liberation. Parimelazhagar: The kural elevates the conquest of anger to the level of spiritual renunciation — mastering temper is mastering the self. Modern Neuroscience: Research on the "amygdala hijack" (Daniel Goleman) confirms that unchecked anger overrides rational judgment — emotional self-regulation is, as the Kural says, a form of inner mastery.

Comparative Philosophy

Seneca	**On Anger — anger is a brief madness that harms the angry more than its target; reason must govern it before it acts.**
Parallel	*Kural 304, 310 — anger as the self-destroying enemy.*
Synthesis	Seneca devoted an entire treatise to the argument that anger is never useful and always corrosive, urging delay and reason as its cure. Thiruvalluvar compresses the same wisdom into two lines: anger is the foremost enemy, and its renunciation is a spiritual victory.

Freedom from Anger in the 21st Century

Emotional intelligence — now recognized as central to leadership, relationships, and mental health — rests on precisely the capacity the Kural exalts: the ability to recognize anger and choose not to be governed by it. In an era of online outrage and reactive escalation, Thiruvalluvar's austere verdict — that anger destroys in seconds what virtue builds over years — has lost none of its force.

பகுதி 4 — PART IV

பொருள் — PORUL: Society and Governance

The Porul section turns from the cultivation of the self to the ordering of society. Between the book's chapters on leadership, governance, justice, and diplomacy, three pillars of statecraft were left unbuilt: the minister and the power of counsel, the ethics of wealth and economy, and the foundations of the strong state. These chapters complete Thiruvalluvar's remarkably modern theory of the well-ordered polity — one in which power is always answerable to virtue.

Chapter 23: Foundations of Leadership

Thiruvalluvar's theory of leadership is among the most sophisticated in ancient thought. Unlike Kautilya's Arthashastra (which counsels' strategic manipulation) or Machiavelli's Prince (which separates ethics from governance), Thiruvalluvar insists that genuine leadership is inseparable from genuine virtue.

குறள் 380 | Kural 380

கண்ணோடாது இட்டான் கணக்கில் தலைமைக்கு பண்ணுவது எல்லாம் அதுவே.

Kannodaadhu ittan kanakil thalaimeiku pannuvadhu ellam adhuve.

Translation: *A ruler who governs without partiality — with neither fear nor favor — sets the standard for true leadership.*

Commentary: Parimelazhagar: Impartiality is the highest administrative virtue. Manakkudavar: A leader who plays favorites destroys the trust that makes governance possible. Kalingar: True leadership treats every case with its merits, not on the relationship. Modern Governance: Max Weber's "bureaucratic ideal" (rational, rule-bound administration) operationalizes this principle. Modern research on procedural justice (Tom Tyler, Yale) shows that people accept unfavorable outcomes when they believe the process was fair.

Leadership Virtues: The Thiruvalluvar Framework

Virtue	Tamil Term	Kural(s)	Modern Leadership Parallel
Courage	வலிமை	382	Authentic leadership; speaking truth to power
Wisdom	அறிவு	381	Evidence-based decision making; epistemic humility
Justice	நீதி	388	Procedural fairness; rule of law
Compassion	அருள்	571	Servant leadership; stakeholder capitalism
Integrity	நேர்மை	655	Ethical leadership; anti-corruption
Vision	தொலைநோக்கு	467	Strategic thinking; long-term planning

Chapter 24: Governance and Political Philosophy

Thiruvalluvar's chapters on governance constitute one of the earliest comprehensive theories of good government in world literature — predating Locke, Montesquieu, and Rousseau by more than fifteen centuries. His framework addresses the ruler's character, the conditions of just governance, the role of advisors, administrative justice, and the relationship between ruler and ruled.

குறள் 541 | Kural 541

அந்தணர் நூலும் அறமும் ஆரா ஒழுகிய நீதிக்கு வாழ்வு ஆதி.

Anthanar nulum araum aara ozhugiya needikku vaazhu aadhi.

Translation: *Justice that flows from knowledge and ethics — that is the foundation of civilized life.*

Commentary: Parimelazhagar: Law without ethics becomes tyranny; ethics without law become chaos. Justice requires both. Manakkudavar: The scholar's learning and the moral person's conduct together provide the dual foundation of just governance. Modern Constitutional Law: The concept of "rule of law" (as opposed to "rule by law") requires that law itself be grounded in ethical principles — precisely Thiruvalluvar's point. International parallel: The UN Declaration of Human Rights grounds legal rights in the inherent dignity of people an ethical, not merely legal, foundation.

குறள் 544 | Kural 544

கோலோச்சும் மன்னவன் கோட்டத்தால் தோன்றும் வேலோச்சும் வேந்தன் வினை.

Koldochum mannavan gottadal thondrum velodochum vendhan vinai.

Translation: *When the ruler's scepter of justice bends — the sword appears; when law fails, violence governs.*

Commentary: This is Thiruvalluvar's most direct political warning: when institutional justice fails, power fills the vacuum. Modern Political Science calls this "democratic backsliding" — the process by which democracies erode as legal institutions lose authority. Contemporary examples: When rule of law weakens in any nation, strongman politics emerges to fill the void. The insight is 2,000 years old; the phenomenon is as contemporary as today's headlines.

Chapter 25 The Minister and the Power of Counsel — அமைச்சும் சொல்வன்மையும்

No ruler governs alone. Thiruvalluvar devotes sustained attention to the minister (amaichu) — the counsellor whose judgment shapes every decision of state. The ideal minister combines a rare set of capacities: the discernment to choose the right means, the right moment, the right method, and the right deed itself. Bound up with this is the power of speech (solvanmai): the ability to advise fearlessly, clearly, and persuasively. Counsel, for the Kural, is where wisdom meets power — and where the fate of nations is often decided.

குறள் 631 | Kural 631

கருவியும் காலமும் செய்கையும் செய்யுமவ் வருவினையும் மாண்டது அமைச்சு.

Karuviyum kaalamum seygaiyum seyyumav; varuvinaiyum maandadhu amaichu.

Translation: *A true minister is one who has mastered the means, the timing, the method, and the difficult deed itself.*

Commentary: Parimelazhagar: The four masteries — means, time, method, and execution — together define the complete counsellor; deficiency in any one disqualifies. Manakkudavar: The minister is judged by capacity for the hard deed, not the easy one. Kalingar: Counsel is an art of discernment — knowing not only what to do but how and when. Modern parallel: This is, in effect, a four-part theory of strategic execution — resources, timing, method, and follow-through — that any contemporary theory of management would recognize.

குறள் 647 | Kural 647

சொலல்வல்லன் சோர்விலன் அஞ்சான் அவனை இகல்வெல்லல் யார்க்கும் அரிது.

Solalvallan sorvilan anjaan avanai; igalvellal yaarkkum aridhu.

Translation: *The one who speaks with power, who never falters, and who knows no fear — him no adversary can overcome.*

Commentary: Parithiyar: Eloquence, stamina, and courage together make the counsellor invincible in debate. Parimelazhagar: The three qualities are cumulative — fluency without courage fails, courage without fluency fails; only their union prevails. Modern application: Studies of effective advocacy and negotiation identify the same triad — clarity of expression, composure under pressure, and the moral courage to speak unwelcome truth — as the core of persuasive influence.

The Four Masteries of Counsel

Mastery	Tamil Sense	Modern Equivalent
The means	karuvi	Resources, instruments, and tools fit for the task
The timing	kaalam	Strategic timing; acting at the decisive moment
The method	seygai	Process design; the right way to execute
The deed	vinai	Execution and follow-through on the hard task

Counsel in the 21st Century

Thiruvalluvar's minister is the ancestor of the modern advisor — the chief of staff, the general counsel, the trusted aide whose judgment a leader relies upon. His warning is timeless: power surrounded by flatterers decays, while power served by fearless, truthful counsel endures. The capacity to tell a leader what they need to hear, clearly and without fear, is as scarce and as vital now as it was two thousand years ago.

Chapter 26 Wealth, Economy, and the Ethics of Prosperity — பொருளும் நாட்டு வளமும்

Thiruvalluvar is no ascetic when it comes to wealth. He treats material prosperity as a genuine good — the engine that makes virtue effective and love secure — provided it is earned by right means. The decisive distinction is ethical, not quantitative: wealth gathered through honest effort, without guile, yields both virtue and joy; wealth gathered by fraud corrupts everything it touches. A prosperous nation, in turn, rests on three foundations — unfailing harvests, worthy people, and merchants of imperishable integrity.

குறள் 754 | Kural 754

அறன்ஈனும் இன்பமும் ஈனும் திறன்அறிந்து தீதின்றி வந்த பொருள்.

Aran eenum inbamum eenum thiran-arindhu; theedhindri vandha porul.

Translation: *Wealth that comes by right means, with skill and without wrong, yields both virtue and joy.*

Commentary: Parimelazhagar: Ethically earned wealth is doubly fruitful — it nourishes both moral and emotional life. Manakkudavar: "Without wrong" is the load-bearing phrase — the manner of acquisition determines the moral character of the wealth. Kalingar: Wealth is not condemned; only its corrupt acquisition is. Modern parallel: The contemporary distinction between value created and value extracted — between wealth that builds and wealth that merely captures — restates Thiruvalluvar's ethical test exactly.

குறள் 731 | Kural 731

தள்ளா விளையுளும் தக்காரும் தாழ்விலாச் செல்வரும் சேர்வது நாடு.

Thallaa vilaiyulum thakkaarum thaazhvilaach; chelvarum servadhu naadu.

Translation: *A true country is one that brings together unfailing harvests, people of worth, and merchants of imperishable integrity.*

Commentary: Parithiyar: A nation's greatness is measured by the union of agricultural abundance, virtuous citizens, and honest commerce. Parimelazhagar: Each of the three is necessary — fertile land without worthy people, or wealth without integrity, cannot sustain a polity. Modern parallel: This is an early model of sustainable national prosperity — food security, human capital, and trustworthy institutions — the very triad development economics now identifies as foundational.

Comparative Philosophy

Aristotle	**Wealth (chrematistike) is instrumental, not an end — good only insofar as it serves the flourishing life.**
Parallel	*Kural 754 — ethically earned wealth as the servant of virtue and joy.*
Synthesis	Aristotle warns against the pursuit of wealth for its own sake while affirming its usefulness for the good life. Thiruvalluvar agrees: prosperity is a real good, but a subordinate one — justified by the virtue and happiness it makes possible, condemned when pursued through wrong.

The Ethics of Prosperity in the 21st Century

Domain	Thiruvalluvar's Principle	Application
Business ethics	Wealth honest in its means	Value creation over extraction; stakeholder capitalism
National economy	Harvests, people, integrity	Food security, human capital, institutional trust
Personal finance	Prosperity that yields virtue	Wealth as a means to a good life, not its goal

Chapter 27: Justice and the Rule of Law — செங்கோல்

The concept of sengol (the scepter of justice) in Thirukkural is not merely a symbol of royal power. It represents the principle of impartial justice — the idea that governance must be measured not by the ruler's will but by the standard of fair treatment for all.

குறள் 550 | Kural 550

அறந்தூக்கும் கோல்போல் மன்னவன் செங்கோல் திறந்தூக்கும் ஒப்பு நிறுத்துப் பார்.

Aran thukkum kolpol mannavan sengol thiranthukkum oppu niruthup paar.

Translation: *The ruler's scepter of justice must stand as perfectly balanced as the scales of dharma — measuring equity in all things.*

Commentary: The scales of justice — Thiruvalluvar's image here has become the universal symbol of law. In Greece, Themis holds the scales; in India's Supreme Court emblem, the scales appear. Thiruvalluvar recorded this image 2,000 years ago. Parimelazhagar: Justice is not the victory of the powerful — it is the calibration of outcomes to merit. Modern jurisprudence: John Rawls's "justice as fairness" (A Theory of Justice, 1971) grounds justice in impartiality — decision-making from behind a "veil of ignorance" about one's social position.

Chapter 28 The Pillars of the State — அரசின் ஆறு உறுப்புகள்

Thiruvalluvar offers one of the oldest systematic theories of national strength in world literature: the doctrine of the six limbs of the state. A complete sovereignty, he holds, possesses army, people, wealth, ministers, allies, and fortification — and the ruler who unites all six is a lion among rulers. This is not a celebration of brute power but an architecture of resilience: each limb checks and supports the others, and the strongest fortress is not the highest wall but the one that is hard to assault, well-provisioned, and easy for its defenders to hold.

குறள் 381 | Kural 381

படைகுடி கூழ்அமைச்சு நட்பரண் ஆறும் உடையான் அரசருள் ஏறு.

Padaikudi koozh-amaichu natparan aarum; udaiyaan arasarul eru.

Translation: *The ruler who possesses all six — army, people, wealth, ministers, allies, and fortress — is a lion among rulers.*

Commentary: Parimelazhagar: The six limbs form an integrated whole; a state strong in five but weak in one is vulnerable through that one. Manakkudavar: "People" (kudi) ranks among the six — the consent and welfare of the governed is itself a pillar of state power. Kalingar: The lion-image marks completeness, not ferocity — the fully constituted state, not the merely aggressive one. Modern parallel: This is an ancient theory of "comprehensive national power," anticipating modern frameworks that combine military, economic, demographic, diplomatic, and institutional strength.

குறள் 745 | Kural 745

கொளற்கரிதாய்க் கொண்டகூழ்த் தாகி அகத்தார் நிலைக்கெளிதாம் நீரது அரண்.

Kolarkaridhaayk konda-koozh thaagi; agattaar nilaikkelidhaam neeradhu aran.

Translation: *A true fortress is one hard to assault, well-stocked with provisions, and easy for those within to defend.*

Commentary: Parithiyar: The three criteria — difficult to attack, well-supplied, and easy to hold — define defensive strength in any age. Parimelazhagar: Provisioning is decisive — a wall that cannot feed its defenders is no fortress at all. Modern parallel: The principles of defensive resilience — hardened against attack, self-sufficient in supply, sustainable for the defender — translate directly into modern thinking on security, from physical infrastructure to cyber-resilience.

The Six Limbs of the State

Limb (Tamil)	Meaning	Modern Equivalent
படை (padai)	Army	Defense and security capacity
குடி (kudi)	People	Citizenry; legitimacy and consent
கூழ் (koozh)	Wealth	Economy and treasury
அமைச்சு (amaichu)	Ministers	Governance and administration
நட்பு (natpu)	Allies	Alliances and diplomacy
அரண் (aran)	Fortress	Infrastructure and defensive resilience

National Strength in the 21st Century

Thiruvalluvar's inclusion of "the people" among the six limbs is quietly revolutionary: long before modern theories of legitimacy, he recognized that a state's strength rests on the welfare and consent of its citizens, not merely on its armies and walls. His balanced model — in which no single source of power suffices alone — reads today as a theory of comprehensive, resilient statecraft, applicable from national security to the design of robust institutions.

Chapter 29: Diplomacy and International Relations

Thirukkural dedicates an entire chapter to the art of the ambassador (thudhu) — a remarkable feature in ancient ethical literature. Thiruvalluvar sees the diplomat not merely as a messenger but as a practitioner of the highest form of ethical communication: speaking truth without fear, reading context with precision, and representing national dignity with grace.

குறள் 690 | Kural 690

கற்றுக்கண் அஞ்சான் செலச்சொல்லி காலத்தால் தக்கது அறிவதாம் தூது.

Katrukkann anjaan selas solli kaalaththaal thakkadhu arivadham thoodhu.

Translation: *Diplomacy is: learning thoroughly, speaking fearlessly and convincingly, knowing the right thing to say at the right time.*

Commentary: Parimelazhagar: The complete diplomat combines four essential qualities — learning (katru), fearlessness (anjaan), clarity of expression (selas solli), and timing (kaalaththaal). Kalingar: Each quality is indispensable; a diplomat with learning but no courage is useless; a diplomat with courage but no learning is dangerous. Modern Diplomatic Training: The World Academy of Art and Science identifies the same four competencies — knowledge, moral courage, communication clarity, and situational awareness — as the core of diplomatic excellence. Joseph Nye's "smart power" concept: effective diplomacy combines hard knowledge with soft communication skills.

பகுதி 5 — PART V

இன்பம் — INBAM: Love and Human Connection

The Inbam section unfolds in two great movements: kalavu, the secret love that precedes union, and karpu, the wedded love that follows it. Between the book's opening chapter on the world of love and its chapter on the psychology of love, these two movements were left unwritten. They are restored here — the trembling birth of desire at first sight, and the mature love of union, separation, sulking, and reunion that culminates in the very last verse of the Kural.

Chapter 30: The World of Love

The Inbam section of Thirukkural is, in many ways, its most remarkable achievement. Most ancient ethical treatises treat love as peripheral to moral life (Stoicism), as a lower pleasure to be regulated (Aristotle), or as an obstacle to liberation (early Buddhism). Only Thirukkural gives love equal standing with virtue and governance — and places it last, signaling that it is the completion, the crowning fulfillment of a good human life.

Thiruvalluvar's treatment of love (inbam) covers 250 kurals — nearly one-fifth of the entire work. This is not romantic indulgence but a serious philosophical claim: a fully human life includes, indeed requires, the experience of deep love and connection.

குறள் 1103 | Kural 1103

அணிகலம் என்பதோர் ஆவதும் இல்லை துணிவு என்பதோர் ஆவதும் இல்லை.

Anikalam enbadhor aavadham illai thunivum enbadhor aavadham illai.

Translation: *Love needs no ornament and requires no courage — it simply is.*

Commentary: Parimelazhagar: True love is not a performance (requiring decoration) nor an achievement (requiring courage) — it is a state of being. Manakkudavar: Love is the natural condition when the right person is met — it requires no effort of will. Kalingar: The attempt to manufacture love through adornment or force reveals its absence. Modern Psychology: Attachment theory (John Bowlby; Mary Ainsworth) identifies "secure attachment" as a state that arises naturally when conditions of safety and reciprocity are present — precisely the effortless quality Thiruvalluvar describes.

குறள் 1286 | Kural 1286

உள்ளினும் தீராப் பெருமகிழ்வு காதலர் கள்ளினும் காட்டுவர் கண்.

Ullinum theeraa perumakizh kaadalar kallinum kaattuvar kann.

Translation: *The beloved's eyes intoxicate more than wine — and even the memory of them brings boundless joy.*

Commentary: Parithiyar: The eyes of the beloved communicate what language cannot — they are the direct window to the inner state of love. Kalingar: The intoxication of wine is external and temporary; the intoxication of love comes from within and transforms perception permanently. Neuroscience (Helen Fisher, Rutgers): Research on the neuroscience of love confirms that the beloved's eyes trigger dopamine release — the neurochemical of pleasure and motivation — creating the sensation of intoxication that Thiruvalluvar describes. The comparison to wine is physiologically accurate.

Chapter 31 Secret Love: The Birth of Desire — களவியல்

The kalavu chapters capture love at its inception — the moment two people meet and the world rearranges itself around a single face. Thiruvalluvar describes, with extraordinary delicacy, the agitation of first attraction, the language of the eyes that speaks what words cannot, and the strange physiology of longing. Here love is not yet social or sanctioned; it is the pure, involuntary upheaval of desire, treated with full dignity and psychological precision. The Kural insists that this experience is not weakness but one of the deepest of human realities.

குறள் 1090 | Kural 1090

உண்டார்கண் அல்லது அடுநறாக் காமம்போல் கண்டார் மகிழ்செய்தல் இன்று.
Undaarkan alladhu adunaraak; kaamampol kandaar magizhseydhal indru.

Translation: *Wine gladdens only those who drink it; but love delights at the very sight of the beloved.*

Commentary: Parimelazhagar: The contrast is exact — wine's joy requires consumption, while love's joy needs only the sight of its object. Manakkudavar: Love is more potent than wine, for it intoxicates through the eyes alone. Kalingar: The very seeing of the beloved is the drinking. Neuroscience (Helen Fisher; Semir Zeki): Research on romantic attraction confirms that the mere sight of a beloved activates the brain's reward circuitry — the "intoxication" Thiruvalluvar describes is, quite literally, a dopaminergic event.

குறள் 1091 | Kural 1091

இருநோக்கு இவளுண்கண் உள்ளது ஒருநோக்கு நோய்நோக்கொன் றந்நோய் மருந்து.
Irunokku ivalunkan ulladhu; orunokku noynokkon randhanoy marundhu.

Translation: *Two glances dwell in her painted eyes: one inflicts the malady of love, and the other is its only cure.*

Commentary: Parithiyar: The beloved's glance both wounds and heals — the same eyes that cause the longing alone can relieve it. Parimelazhagar: This paradox — the cause and the cure united in one source — is the essence of love's helpless condition. Modern Psychology: Attachment research describes precisely this dynamic — the attachment figure is simultaneously the source of distress in separation and the source of comfort in reunion.

Comparative Reflection

Sangam Akam Tradition	**Love sung from the lovers' own voices — the inner landscape of desire given full literary dignity.**
Parallel	*Kural 1090, 1091 — the agitation and language of first love.*
Synthesis	Thiruvalluvar writes within the Tamil akam tradition, in which the interior experience of love — its trembling, its glances, its sleeplessness — is treated as serious subject matter. Unlike traditions that subordinate romantic love to duty or treat it as a distraction from the higher life, the Kural grants it equal philosophical standing.

The Birth of Desire in the 21st Century

Modern neuroscience has only recently caught up with what Thiruvalluvar described two millennia ago: that romantic attraction is a distinct neurochemical state, that the sight of a beloved triggers measurable reward responses, and that longing has a physiology of its own. The Kural's achievement is to render these states not clinically but humanely — honoring the experience of falling in love as one of the central facts of being human.

Chapter 32: The Psychology of Love

In the later chapters of the Inbam section, Thiruvalluvar plunges into the psychology of love with remarkable precision. Love here is not merely an emotion but a complete psychological phenomenon — encompassing identity, memory, longing, pain, and joy. The kurals on love psychology anticipate modern neuroscience by two millennia.

குறள் 1279 | Kural 1279

உள்ளக்கலந்த உயிரினும் நன்றே கிளைக் கலந்த நட்பு.

Ullak kalantha uyirinum nanre killak kalantha natpu.

Translation: *The friendship that has mingled with the heart is greater even than one's own life.*

Commentary: This kural captures love at its deepest psychological moment: the beloved's life becomes more valuable than one's own. Parimelazhagar: This is not romantic exaggeration — it describes the actual phenomenology of deep love, in which self-interest gives way to care for the other. Modern Psychology: John Gottman's longitudinal research on lasting relationships identifies this "other-focused" quality — valuing the partner's flourishing above one's own comfort — as the hallmark of secure, lasting love. Attachment Theory: "Secure attachment" (Bowlby) is precisely this state of mutual cherishing.

Chapter 33 Wedded Love: Union, Sulking, and Reunion — கற்பியல்

The karpu chapters portray love in its mature, enduring form — the love of those who have united and must now navigate separation, longing, and the subtle drama of the lovers' quarrel. Thiruvalluvar's genius here lies in his treatment of oodal: the feigned sulking between lovers that, far from threatening their bond, deepens it. The Kural's very last verse declares that sulking, reconciliation, and reunion are themselves the rewards of love — ending the entire 1,330-verse work not on duty or governance, but on the renewing joy of human intimacy.

குறள் 1267 | Kural 1267

புலப்பேன்கொல் புல்லுவேன் கொல்லோ கலப்பேன்கொல் கண்அன்ன கேளிர் விடின்.

Pulappenkol pulluvenkollo kalappenkol; kan-anna kelir vidin.

Translation: *When my beloved, dear as my own eyes, returns — shall I sulk, or embrace, or do both at once?*

Commentary: Parimelazhagar: The lover is torn between the wish to punish the absence with a sulk and the longing to embrace — a perfect portrait of love's sweet confusion. Manakkudavar: The very impulse to sulk is itself a sign of love's depth. Kalingar: "Dear as my own eyes" measures the love against the most precious of faculties. Modern Psychology: This ambivalence — the simultaneous wish to protest and to reconnect after separation — is exactly the reunion behavior attachment theory documents in securely bonded pairs.

குறள் 1330 | Kural 1330

ஊடல் உணர்தல் புணர்தல் இவைகாமம் கூடியார் பெற்ற பயன்.

Oodal unardhal punardhal ivai-kaamam; koodiyaar petra payan.

Translation: *Sulking, reconciliation, and the renewal of union — these are the very rewards that lovers reap from love.*

Commentary: This is the final kural of the entire Thirukkural — the last of 1,330 verses. Parimelazhagar: The work ends not on austerity but on the living rhythm of intimate love — protest, understanding, and renewed union. Parithiyar: The lovers' quarrel is not a flaw in love but one of its fruits. Kalingar: That Thiruvalluvar chose to close his vast ethical edifice on this note is itself a philosophical statement — the fully human life is fulfilled in love. Modern reading: To end a treatise on virtue, governance, and ethics with the sweetness of reconciliation is to declare that all the disciplines of the good life finally serve the flourishing of human connection.

Comparative Philosophy

Aristotle / Modern Psychology	**Eudaimonia and secure attachment — the complete life is fulfilled in enduring, reciprocal bonds.**
Parallel	*Kural 1267, 1330 love's mature rhythm of separation, sulking, and reunion.*
Synthesis	Where Aristotle locates the crown of the good life in friendship and shared activity, and modern attachment theory locates flourishing in secure, responsive bonds, Thiruvalluvar places the seal of his entire work on wedded love — the daily, renewing intimacy that survives quarrel and absence. All three agree: the good life is, in the end, a life of deep connection.

Wedded Love in the 21st Century

Relationship science has discovered what the Kural assumed: that conflict, handled well, strengthens rather than weakens a bond. John Gottman's research identifies the capacity to repair after conflict — to move from rupture back to closeness — as the single strongest predictor of lasting love. Thiruvalluvar's oodal, the sulk that ends in reconciliation, is precisely this repair process, recognized as a source of joy rather than a threat. The Kural ends, fittingly, with the wisdom that to quarrel and reconcile is itself one of love's deepest pleasures.

பகுதி 6 — PART VI

Debates and Controversies

Chapter 34: Is Thirukkural a Religious Text?

Thirukkural opens with a chapter called "Kataavul Vaazhthu" (Praise of God) — but the deity praised is described in terms so broadly philosophical that no single religious tradition can claim exclusive ownership. This is not ambiguity or confusion; it is a deliberate philosophical position.

Religious Interpretation	Key Evidence	Proponents	Critical Assessment
Hindu (Shaiva)	"Aadhi Bhagavan" = Shiva/Vishnu; ahimsa and karma concepts	Parimelazhagar; modern Tamil Hindus	Reads specific divinity into deliberately open language
Jainism	Complete ahimsa; self-discipline; no Creator God; rejection of animal sacrifice	Parithiyar; G.U. Pope noted Jain influences	Strong textual support for Jain ethical framework
Secular/Universal	No specific God, ritual, or reincarnation doctrine required	Modern Tamil rationalists; Periyar tradition	Consistent with text; may underestimate spiritual dimension
Buddhism	Compassion (arul) as central virtue; ahimsa	Some Western scholars	Weaker support than Jain parallel; no explicit Buddhist cosmology

> *"The deliberate ambiguity of Thirukkural's first chapter is not a weakness — it is its greatest philosophical strength. Thiruvalluvar created a text that every civilization could claim as its own, because it addresses what every civilization shares: the challenge of living well."*
>
> **— Kamil Zvelebil, Tamil Literature**

Chapter 35: Gender and Thirukkural

The gender dimensions of Thirukkural are among its most discussed aspects in contemporary scholarship. The text contains both advanced elements — treating female desire and pain with full human dignity in the Inbam section — and historically bounded elements that reflect the social norms of its time.

Progressive Elements

- The Inbam section is primarily written from a female speaker's perspective (following Sangam akam tradition), granting women's inner life equal ethical weight.
- Kural 56 declares that a wife of good character is more powerful than any ascetic — granting women ethical authority.
- Love in the Inbam section is mutual — both partners' emotions are treated as equally significant.

Historically Bounded Elements

- Some Porul chapters reflect patriarchal household assumptions typical of the period.
- Certain chapters on the courtesan (vilamahu) have been subject to feminist critique regarding the objectification of women.

The most nuanced contemporary reading holds both: that Thirukkural's universal ethical principles transcend its historical gender arrangements, and that honest engagement requires acknowledging where the text reflects its historical limitations. This scholarly honesty enhances, rather than diminishes, the text's credibility as a guide to human life.

Chapter 36 Caste, Equality, and Social Justice in Thirukkural

Among the most consequential debates in Thirukkural scholarship is the question of social hierarchy. Does the Kural endorse the hereditary divisions of its age, or does it transcend them? The evidence points decisively toward a radical egalitarianism rare in any ancient text. Thiruvalluvar declares plainly that all human beings are equal by birth — that the only meaningful distinctions among people arise from their actions, not their ancestry. This single principle has made the Kural a touchstone for social-justice movements across two millennia.

குறள் 972 | Kural 972

பிறப்பொக்கும் எல்லா உயிர்க்கும் சிறப்பொவ்வா செய்தொழில் வேற்றுமை யான்.

Pirappokkum ellaa uyirkkum; sirappovvaa seydhozhil vetrumai yaan.

Translation: *All living beings are equal in birth; differences in dignity arise only from the differences in what they do.*

Commentary: Parimelazhagar: Birth confers no superiority — every human being enters the world on equal footing; only conduct and occupation create distinction. Manakkudavar: "Equal in birth" is stated without qualification — a direct repudiation of inherited rank. Kalingar: Dignity is earned through action, never inherited through lineage. Modern parallel: This is, in essence, the principle later enshrined in modern human-rights doctrine — that all persons are born equal in dignity, and that worth is a matter of conduct, not caste.

குறள் 973 | Kural 973

மேலிருந்தும் மேலல்லார் மேலல்லர் கீழிருந்தும் கீழல்லார் கீழல் லவர்.

Melirundhum melallaar melallar; keezhirundhum keezhallaar keezhal lavar.

Translation: *The high-placed who lack nobility are not truly high; the low-placed who are not base are not truly low.*

Commentary: Parithiyar: Social position and moral worth are entirely separable — rank does not confer nobility, nor does humble station confer baseness. Parimelazhagar: True elevation is of character, not of station. Kalingar: The kural inverts the social order of its time, locating real height and lowness in conduct alone. Modern reading: This is a frontal challenge to any system that equates inherited status with human worth — a claim as relevant to contemporary debates on privilege and meritocracy as to the caste hierarchies of antiquity.

The Scholarly Debate

Three positions structure the modern discussion. The first holds that the Kural is fundamentally egalitarian, with verses like 972 and 973 representing its core ethical vision — a text that, properly read, dissolves the basis of caste. A second position notes that certain Porul chapters reflect the social arrangements of their period, and cautions against anachronistically projecting modern equality onto an ancient text. The third, and most widely held among contemporary scholars, holds both truths at once: that Thiruvalluvar's universal ethical principles transcend the social hierarchies of his time, even where the text occasionally reflects them, and that this honest reading strengthens rather than weakens the Kural's moral authority

Comparative Philosophy

Modern Human Rights	**All human beings are born free and equal in dignity and rights (UDHR, Article 1).**
Parallel	*Kural 972 — equality of birth; dignity from deeds, not descent.*
Synthesis	The opening article of the Universal Declaration of Human Rights states what Kural 972 stated two thousand years earlier: that human equality is a fact of birth, and that distinctions of worth must be earned through conduct, never assigned by lineage. The convergence is striking — an ancient Tamil verse anticipating the founding principle of modern rights.

Social Justice in the 21st Century

The Kural's principle — equality by birth, distinction by deed — has been invoked by reformers and social-justice movements across the centuries precisely because it provides an internal, indigenous basis for equality, drawn from one of Tamil civilization's most revered texts. In contemporary debates over caste, privilege, and meritocracy, Thiruvalluvar's verses remain a living resource: a two-thousand-year-old declaration that no human being is born superior to another, and that what we do, not where we come from, is the true measure of our dignity.

பகுதி 7 — PART VII

Science, Technology, and Modern Life

Chapter 37: Thirukkural and Artificial Intelligence

The rise of artificial intelligence raises ethical questions that ancient wisdom traditions were not explicitly designed to address. Yet the human values that determine whether AI becomes beneficial or harmful are precisely the values Thirukkural has always examined. The question is not whether Thiruvalluvar anticipated AI — he did not. The question is whether his ethical framework provides guidance for the humans designing, deploying, and governing AI systems. It does, profoundly.

The AI Ethics Crisis: A Summary

As of 2024-2026, AI development faces several interconnected ethical challenges: algorithmic bias in hiring, criminal sentencing, and healthcare; autonomous weapons systems without adequate human oversight; AI-generated misinformation at scale; labor displacement without social safety nets; concentration of AI capability in a small number of corporations; and the emerging challenge of superintelligent AI alignment.

Each of these challenges has a direct parallel in Thirukkural's ethical framework — not because Thiruvalluvar predicted AI, but because each challenge is fundamentally a question of human values: fairness, accountability, truth, compassion, and the wise use of power.

AI Ethics Framework Derived from Thirukkural

AI Ethics Principle	Relevant Kural(s)	Thiruvalluvar's Insight	Modern AI Application
Truth and Accuracy	291, 423	False speech corrupts the speaker and harms the listener	AI systems must not generate or amplify misinformation; hallucination in LLMs is a truth violation
Non-harm (Ahimsa)	241, 321	Reducing harm to all living beings is the foundation of ethics	Safety-first AI development; rigorous risk assessment before deployment
Accountability	661	Power requires responsibility; those who act must answer for consequences	Human oversight of AI decisions; explainable AI; audit trails
Fairness and Justice	541, 547	Justice weighs all parties equally; bias corrupts justice	Algorithmic fairness; bias testing across demographic groups
Precautionary Thinking	467	Consider carefully before acting; irreversible decisions demand extra care	AI safety research; staged deployment; reversibility planning
Transparency	293, 294	Secrecy and deception corrupt trust in all relationships	AI transparency requirements; disclosure of AI-generated content
Human Welfare Priority	571	Governance exists to serve the governed, not the governor	Human-centered AI design; AI must benefit users, not just creators
Long-term Thinking	671	The wise person considers consequences beyond the immediate moment	AGI alignment; avoiding short-term optimization that creates long-term catastrophe

Deep Dive: AI Safety and Kural 467

குறள் 467 | Kural 467

அழிவினும் ஆக்கம் பெரிதெனினும் ஆகா வழியில் செலவிடா தொழுக்கு.

Azivinum aakkam peridininum aaga vazhiyil selavidaa tozhukkam.

Translation: *Even if the gain seems greater than the loss, do not pursue it through improper means.*

Commentary: Parimelazhagar: The ends do not justify the means — a principle Thiruvalluvar states with unusual directness. Manakkudavar: If the process is corrupted, the gain is corrupted. AI Safety Parallel: This is precisely the problem of "reward hacking" in AI — systems that maximize their objective function through unintended means, achieving the measured goal while violating the intended purpose. The alignment problem in AI is, at its core, the problem Kural 467 identifies: optimizing for stated metrics while ignoring the underlying values those metrics were meant to proxy.

Deep Dive: Algorithmic Justice and Kural 541

Modern algorithmic decision systems in criminal sentencing (COMPAS), hiring (Amazon's recruitment AI), facial recognition, and medical diagnosis have all demonstrated systematic bias against marginalized groups. Thiruvalluvar's concept of sengol (the balanced scales of justice) directly addresses this: justice that tilts toward those with power is not justice.

> *"The scholar's knowledge and the moral person's conduct are the foundation of justice — not the ruler's preference or convenience."*
> **— Kural 541 (Thiruvalluvar)**

Applied to AI: Algorithmic systems trained predominantly on data from privileged populations will systematically underserve marginalized ones. The correction requires not just technical fixes but a commitment to the principle of Kural 541: the output of any justice-relevant system must be calibrated to treat all people as having equal worth.

Explainable AI and the Virtue of Transparency

One of the central debates in contemporary AI ethics concerns "black box" systems — AI models that produce outputs without comprehensible reasoning. The European Union's AI Act mandates "explainability" for high-stakes AI decisions. Thiruvalluvar would recognize this as a straightforward application of his principle of truth (vaymai): if you cannot explain how you reached a conclusion, you cannot claim it is true.

- Kural 423: "Test by reason before accepting; reason that does not survive examination cannot be knowledge."
- Application: AI systems making high-stakes decisions (parole, medical diagnosis, credit) must be interpretable by those affected.
- The "right to explanation" in the EU GDPR is Kural 423 operationalized in law.

AGI Alignment and Kural 34

The deepest challenge in AI safety — the alignment problem for superintelligent AI — parallels Kural 34's insight about mental purity. A superintelligent AI with misaligned values is more dangerous than one with lesser capability. The capability must emerge from aligned values, not be applied in service of misaligned ones. Thiruvalluvar's principle: virtue begins in the mind (inner alignment) and then manifests in action (external behavior). AGI safety requires exactly this sequence.

Chapter 38: Environment and Sustainability

Rain — The Center of Thiruvalluvar's Environmental Ethics

Environmental ethics in Thirukkural is not a separate section — it is woven into the deepest foundation of the text. Immediately after the opening invocation, Thiruvalluvar addresses rain. This is not coincidence. Rain (mazhai) in Thirukkural represents the gift of life itself — the indispensable condition for all human flourishing, all virtue, all governance, all love.

குறள் 11 | Kural 11

வானின்று உலகம் வழங்கி வருதலான் தான் அமிழ்தம் என்றுணர்க மழை.

Vaanindru ulagam vazhagi varuthalan thaan amizhdham endrunkura mazhai.

Translation: *Since the world subsists by rain that comes from the sky — understand rain as ambrosia itself.*

Commentary: Parimelazhagar: Ambrosia (amizhdham) is what sustains the gods' immortality in mythology. Rain is described as the equivalent — it sustains human civilization's continuation. Manakkudavar: The comparison elevates rain from natural phenomenon to ethical concern: that which sustains all life is sacred and must be protected. Modern parallels: The UN's Sustainable Development Goal 6 (Clean Water and Sanitation) and Goal 13 (Climate Action) are policy manifestations of the principle Thiruvalluvar stated in Kural 11. Planetary Boundaries framework (Rockström et al.): freshwater use is one of nine planetary boundaries whose violation threatens civilizational stability.

குறள் 18 | Kural 18

சிறப்பொடு பூசனை செல்லாது வானம் வறக்குமேல் வானோர்க்கும் ஈண்டு.

Sirappodu poodsanai selladu vaanam varakkumel vaanorkum eendu.

Translation: *If the sky dries up — if rain fails — even the festivals of the gods will cease.*

Commentary: This is Thiruvalluvar's most radical environmental statement: if the water cycle fails, religion itself fails. Nature is not subservient to culture or religion — culture and religion are dependent on nature. This anticipates the core insight of modern environmental philosophy: the "natural capital" on which all human enterprise depends. Herman Daly's ecological economics and Kate Raworth's "doughnut economics" both ground economic and social activity within ecological limits — precisely the insight of Kural 18.

குறள் 20 | Kural 20

நீரின்று அமையாது உலகெனின் யார்யார்க்கும் வானின்று அமையாது ஒழுக்கு.

Neerinru amaiyadu ulageninil yaaryaarkum vaanindru amaiyadu ozhukkam.

Translation: *If the world cannot function without water — then for all living beings, no ethical life is possible without rain.*

Commentary: The phrase "yaaryaarkum" (for all, whoever they may be) is crucial: Thiruvalluvar includes not just humans but all sentient beings in the circle of dependency on water. This is ecocentrism — the recognition that ethical consideration must extend beyond humanity to the ecosystems on which all life depends. Modern parallels: Leopold's Land Ethic (A Sand County Almanac, 1949): "A thing is right when it tends to preserve the integrity, stability, and beauty of the biotic community." Thiruvalluvar stated this in seven words 1,700 years earlier.

Climate Crisis — Thiruvalluvar's Warning Made Manifest

The IPCC Sixth Assessment Report (2021-2023) documents what Thiruvalluvar warned: disrupting the water cycle — through deforestation, fossil fuel combustion, and industrial pollution — creates cascading civilizational crises. Today, 2.5 billion people face water scarcity; the number is projected to reach 5.7 billion by 2050. Agricultural systems that have fed humanity for millennia are failing. Ocean acidification threatens marine food chains.

Thirukkural Principle	Kural	Contemporary Crisis	Policy Response
Rain sustains all civilization	11	Water scarcity affects 2.5B people	UN SDG 6: Clean Water for All
Water enables all ethics	20	Water wars emerging globally	International water governance treaties
Nature precedes religion/culture	18	Climate-driven migration and conflict	Paris Agreement; Green New Deal
Agriculture is foundational	1033	Soil degradation threatens food security	Regenerative agriculture policies
All beings depend on water	20	Biodiversity collapse from water stress	Convention on Biological Diversity

Circular Economy and Thirukkural

The concept of a circular economy — one in which waste is eliminated through cycling of materials back into the production system — reflects Thiruvalluvar's deep understanding of ecological interdependence. In the rain cycle (Kurals 11–20), every element is recycled: rain nourishes soil, soil produces food, food sustains life, life honors rain. This is the original circular economy.

- Ellen MacArthur Foundation's Circular Economy principles: eliminate waste, circulate materials, regenerate nature.
- Thirukkural parallel: "The world functions through the cycle of rain" (Kural 11) — nature's circular system is the model for all sustainable human systems.
- Regenerative Agriculture: rebuilding soil through composting and cover cropping mirrors the rain-soil-crop cycle Thiruvalluvar celebrates.

Chapter 39: Business Ethics

Stakeholder Capitalism — The Kural View

Thirukkural's analysis of ethical wealth-creation aligns with the contemporary movement toward "stakeholder capitalism" — the view that corporations have obligations not only to shareholders but to employees, customers, communities, and the natural environment. Milton Friedman's 1970 doctrine ("the social responsibility of business is to increase its profits") has been progressively challenged; Thiruvalluvar challenged it 2,000 years earlier.

குறள் 754 | Kural 754

அல்லல் பருவத்தும் ஆற்றும் அரும் துணை சொல்லிழுக்கா நட்பு.

Allal parvathum aarum aram thunai sollizhukka natpu.

Translation: *The friendship that endures through times of hardship without failing in speech or deed — that is the true ally.*

Commentary: Business Ethics application: A business that treats employees, suppliers, and communities as genuine partners — not merely as inputs to be optimized — is practicing Thiruvalluvar's principle of true friendship (natpu) in commercial life. The collapse of Enron, Theranos, and countless other corporations can be traced to the violation of this principle: relationships treated as transactional rather than genuine. Comparative: Robert Greenleaf's servant leadership and Freeman's stakeholder theory both operationalize the kind of genuine partnership Thiruvalluvar describes.

Business Ethics Principle	Kural Basis	Modern Application	Case Study
Transparency	293, 294	Accurate financial reporting; no greenwashing	Patagonia's genuine environmental commitments vs. "eco-washing"
Stakeholder accountability	388, 541	ESG reporting; B-Corporation certification	Unilever's "Sustainable Living Plan" commitment to all stakeholders
Ethical wealth creation	754, 659	Fair wages; sustainable supply chains	Living wage initiatives; Fairtrade certification
Long-term thinking	467, 671	Rejecting short-termism; sustainable investment	Unilever vs. Kraft Heinz hostile takeover (long-term vs. short-term value)
Employee dignity	521, 571	Fair wages; workplace dignity; mental health	Costco's above-market wages reducing turnover and increasing productivity

Chapter 40: Education and Lifelong Learning

Thiruvalluvar's chapters on knowledge (arivu) and learning constitute one of the most sophisticated ancient treatments of education as a lifelong philosophical practice. Unlike systems that treat education as credential-acquisition, Thiruvalluvar defines learning as the transformation of character and the capacity for wise action.

குறள் 391 | Kural 391

கற்க கசடறக் கற்பவை கற்றபின் நிற்க அதற்குத் தக.

Karka kasadara karpavai katrapin nirka adharku thaga.

Translation: *Learn thoroughly what ought to be learned — and after learning, live accordingly.*

Commentary: Parimelazhagar: "Kasadara" (without residue, without defect) specifies the quality of learning required: comprehensive, thorough, leaving no gaps. Manakkudavar: True learning is not accumulation of information — it is transformation of character. The test of learning is not the examination passed but the life lived. Kalingar: Thiruvalluvar identifies learning and living as a single integrated process — understanding that does not change action is not understanding. Modern Learning Science: The concept of "deep learning" (as opposed to "surface learning") in educational psychology aligns perfectly: deep learning involves structural change in understanding, not memorization of facts. Bloom's Taxonomy: the highest level of learning is "creation" — generating new knowledge from understanding. Thiruvalluvar identifies the highest level as "living accordingly."

குறள் 400 | Kural 400

கேடில் விழுச்செல்வம் கல்வி ஒருவற்கு மாடல்ல மற்றை யவை.

Kedil vizhuselvam kalvi oruvadrku madalla matrai yavai.

Translation: *Knowledge is the imperishable supreme wealth; no other wealth can match it.*

Commentary: Parithiyar: Material wealth can be stolen, lost, taxed, or devalued. Knowledge invested in the mind cannot be taken. Kalingar: The metaphor of wealth is apt: knowledge compounds over time, just as invested capital does. Modern Knowledge Economy: The World Bank and OECD consistently find that human capital — measured by educational attainment and cognitive skills — is the primary driver of economic development. Countries that invest in education consistently outperform those that do not. Thiruvalluvar's principle is now a cornerstone of development economics.

Learning Science and Thirukkural: Modern Parallels

Educational Concept	Thirukkural Principle	Modern Research Parallel
Deep vs. Surface Learning	Kural 391: Learn without residue, then live accordingly	Marton & Saljo (1976): deep learning creates structural change; surface learning is temporary retention
Knowledge Transfer	Kural 393: Use learning in practice	OECD PISA framework: applied knowledge transfer as highest educational goal
Lifelong Learning	Kural 400: Knowledge is imperishable wealth	World Economic Forum: lifelong learning as essential adaptation skill for 21st century labor market
Epistemic Humility	Kural 423: Reason before accepting; test all claims	Carl Sagan's "baloney detection kit"; scientific literacy as foundation of citizenship
Moral Education	Kural 34: Mental purity precedes virtue	Character education movement (Lickona): virtue must be cultivated, not merely explained

பகுதி 8 — PART VIII

Thirukkural in the World

Chapter 41: Global Reception and Translation History

Language Region	Key Languages	Notable Editions/Translators
Western Europe	English, French, German, Spanish	G.U. Pope (1886), P.S. Sundaram (1990), T.N. Ramachandran, Pruiksma (2014)
Eastern Europe	Russian, Polish, Czech	Russian Academy of Sciences edition; Soviet-era interest
East Asia	Mandarin, Japanese, Korean	Modern academic editions; growing scholarly interest
South Asia	Sanskrit, Hindi, Telugu, Kannada, Malayalam	Multiple editions; some pre-colonial translations
Middle East	Arabic, Persian, Turkish	Modern translations; growing academic interest
Africa	Swahili, selected national languages	Digital expansion currently driving new translations
Total	80+ languages	UNESCO World Heritage designation; ongoing digital translation projects

Chapter 42 Thirukkural in Public Life: Education, Politics, and Popular Culture

A text endures not only on the shelves of scholars but in the living practice of a people. Thirukkural is woven into the public life of the Tamil world to a degree few classical works anywhere can match. It is recited in schools and inscribed in legislatures, quoted by politicians of every persuasion, cited in courtrooms, printed on coins and government documents, and carried in the memory of ordinary people who can summon a kural for nearly any occasion. This chapter traces how a two-thousand-year-old work of seven-word verses became, and remains, a part of daily civic and cultural life.

குறள் 397 | Kural 397

யாதானும் நாடாமால் ஊராமால் என்னொருவன் சாந்துணையுங் கல்லாத வாறு.

Yaadhaanum naadaamaal ooraamaal; ennoruvan saandhunaiyung kallaadha vaaru.

Translation: *Since the learned find every land their land and every town their town, why would anyone neglect to learn for as long as they live?*

Commentary: Parimelazhagar: Learning makes the whole world one's home — the educated belong everywhere. Manakkudavar: Knowledge dissolves the boundaries of place; the learned are citizens of all lands. Kalingar: The kural makes lifelong learning a near-obligation, given its universal passport. Modern parallel: In a globalized, knowledge-driven world, this verse reads as a charter for both lifelong learning and global citizenship — education as the universal language that opens every door.

In Education

- Thirukkural verses are part of school curricula across Tamil-speaking regions, memorized by generations of students as a foundation of moral and linguistic education.
- Its compact, two-line form makes it uniquely teachable — a complete ethical lesson that can be learned, recited, and carried for life in a single breath.
- Universities and research institutions worldwide study the Kural as literature, philosophy, and comparative ethics, sustaining a scholarly tradition over a thousand years old.

In Politics and Public Institutions

- Leaders and legislators across the political spectrum quote the Kural to lend moral weight to their arguments — a rare instance of a classical text that all sides claim.
- Its verses on justice, leadership, and good governance are invoked in public debate, ceremonial occasions, and official discourse.

- The Kural's deliberate refusal to bind itself to any one religion or political system is precisely what allows it to serve as common ethical ground for a diverse public.

In Popular Culture and Daily Life

- Kurals appear in film dialogue, song, oratory, journalism, and everyday conversation — a living idiom rather than a museum piece.
- The text has been translated into more than eighty languages and recognized internationally, carrying Tamil ethical thought to a global audience.
- Among the Tamil diaspora across the world, the Kural functions as a portable homeland — a compact carrier of cultural identity and shared values.

Comparative Reflection

World Classics in Public Life	**Few classical texts — Confucius' Analects, perhaps — remain so embedded in the everyday civic and cultural life of a living people.**
Parallel	*Kural 397 — learning as the universal passport.*
Synthesis	Like the Analects in East Asia, Thirukkural functions in the Tamil world not as a relic but as a living public scripture — quoted, taught, inscribed, and lived. Its endurance in daily life, across two millennia and now across the globe, is itself the strongest testimony to the universality its author intended.

Thirukkural in the World Today

That a work of 1,330 verses, composed two thousand years ago, should remain a fixture of classrooms, legislatures, courtrooms, films, and ordinary conversation is a phenomenon almost without parallel in world literature. The Kural's presence in public life is not the result of official imposition but of voluntary, continuous reuse by a people who keep finding it relevant. As the text travels further — into new languages, new media, and the global Tamil diaspora — it continues to do what Thiruvalluvar designed it to do: to speak, in seven words at a time, to the permanent questions of human life.

Chapter 43: Why Thirukkural Endures

The Secret of 2,000 Years of Relevance

Most ancient texts become increasingly inaccessible as their historical context recedes. Thirukkural speaks directly to readers across two millennia. Why?

- Universality of Ethical Questions: Thirukkural addresses permanent features of human existence — the need for truth, the challenge of power, the complexity of love — rather than historically specific problems.
- Economy of Expression: 1,330 kurals can be memorized in their entirety. This compressibility has made the text resilient to cultural transmission losses.
- Deliberate Openness: By refusing to embed its ethics in a specific theology or political system, Thiruvalluvar created a text that every civilization could claim as its own.
- Literary Beauty: The kurals are not only wise — they are beautiful. The compression of profound ideas into seven words demands and rewards rereading.
- Range: From personal virtue to diplomacy to environmental ethics to love — Thirukkural addresses the full spectrum of human concerns, making it relevant at every stage of life.

பகுதி 9 — PART IX (NEW)

Thirukkural and World Philosophy

Chapters 44–48

Chapter 44: Thirukkural and Aristotle

Two Founders of Ethical Thought Across Two Civilizations

Aristotle (384–322 BCE) and Thiruvalluvar (approximately 1st century BCE to 2nd century CE) represent two of the greatest systematic thinkers in human history. Writing in different languages, on different continents, for different audiences — they arrived at remarkably convergent conclusions about human excellence, political life, and the conditions of flourishing.

Theme	Aristotle (Nicomachean Ethics)	Thiruvalluvar (Thirukkural)	Convergence Point
Virtue	Virtue as stable character disposition (hexis); achieved through practice	Virtue begins in mental purity (Kural 34); expressed in consistent conduct	Both: virtue is a state, not an act; character precedes behavior
Leadership	The politician must possess practical wisdom (phronesis) + moral virtue	The king must be wise, courageous, just, and compassionate (Kural 382-388)	Both: Leadership is the integration of wisdom and virtue — neither alone suffices
Justice	Justice is proportionate equality; corrective and distributive	Justice (sengol) weighs all equally; corrects imbalance (Kural 541, 550)	Both: justice is calibrated fairness, not mere equality of treatment
Human Flourishing	Eudaimonia: flourishing through excellent activity over a complete life	Aram → Porul → Inbam: ethical life fulfilled in love — complete human flourishing	Both: the good life is whole-life excellence across multiple domains
Friendship	Three types: utility, pleasure, virtue — only virtue friendship is complete	True friendship endures hardship (Kural 786, 788); tested by adversity	Both: genuine friendship requires shared virtue, not merely shared interest

> *"The remarkable thing is not that Aristotle and Thiruvalluvar reached similar conclusions — but that they did so independently, in different cultural contexts, addressing different audiences, suggesting that their shared insights track something true about human nature itself."*
>
> **— Dr. Perumal Pugazhendhi**

Chapter 45: Thirukkural and Confucius

Ethics of Social Harmony — East and South

Confucius (551–479 BCE) and Thiruvalluvar both built ethical systems centered on the cultivation of human relationships as the foundation of social order. Both rejected purely legalistic governance and insisted that virtue must be cultivated from within, not merely enforced from without.

Theme	Confucius (Analects)	Thiruvalluvar (Thirukkural)	Divergence
Family	Filial piety (xiao) is the root of all virtue; family order mirrors cosmic order	Family (illaram) is the training ground for social virtue (Kural 41-60)	Confucius: family is the foundation of state. Thiruvalluvar: family is one of three equal pillars (aram, porul, inbam)
Governance	Ruler must embody ren (benevolence) to transform society by example	Ruler's virtue inspires subjects; corruption corrupts society (Kural 388)	Both: governance through moral example, not coercion. Confucius: ritual; Thiruvalluvar: inner virtue
Education	Anyone can learn virtue; social class does not determine capacity for learning	Knowledge is the greatest wealth; available to all (Kural 400)	Both: education as democratizing force. Confucius emphasized ritual learning; Thiruvalluvar emphasized practical wisdom
Social Harmony	Ren (benevolence) creates social harmony through hierarchical relationships	Virtue creates harmony through inner transformation and just governance	Confucius: harmony through proper role fulfillment. Thiruvalluvar: harmony through ethical equality

Chapter 46: Thirukkural and Stoicism

Self-Mastery as the Foundation of the Good Life

The Stoic philosophers — Zeno of Citium (344–262 BCE), Epictetus (50–135 CE), Marcus Aurelius (121–180 CE), Seneca (4 BCE–65 CE) — built one of the ancient world's most influential ethical systems around the concept of self-mastery: the idea that the truly free person is one who governs their responses to the world, not one who simply accumulates power or pleasure.

Stoic Concept	Stoic Teaching	Thirukkural Parallel	Kural Reference
Prohairesis (rational choice)	Freedom lies in mastering one's judgments and impulses	Self-discipline (adakkam) is the highest human capacity	Kural 121-130
Apatheia (non-passion)	Negative emotions arise from false judgments; the sage is undisturbed	Non-anger (vegulaamai): anger destroys in moments what virtue builds over years	Kural 301-310
Logos (rational nature)	Living according to reason and nature is the highest good	Truth (vaymai) and mental purity (Kural 34) as alignment with reality	Kural 291, 34
Oikeiosis (kinship)	Expanding circle of concern from self to family to all humanity	Compassion (arul) extends to all living beings, not merely humans	Kural 241, 321
Memento Mori (remembering death)	Impermanence focuses attention on what truly matters	Impermanence (nilayaamai): understanding impermanence motivates ethical urgency	Kural 331-340
Amor Fati (love of fate)	Acceptance of what cannot be changed; focus on what can be	Patience (poraiyudaimai): bearing what must be borne with dignity	Kural 151-160

> *"You have power over your mind — not outside events. Realize this, and you will find strength."*
> **— Marcus Aurelius, Meditations**

குறள் 158 | Kural 158

பொறுத்தல் இறைவற்கு அணி.

Poruththal iraivarku ani.

Translation: *Patience is the ornament of those in power.*

Commentary: Marcus Aurelius and Thiruvalluvar — separated by more than a century and half the world — arrive at the identical conclusion: the measure of power is not how swiftly one can retaliate, but how gracefully one can endure. The Meditations (Book II) and Kural 158 could have been written in conversation.

Chapter 47: Thirukkural and Buddhism

Compassion, Nonviolence, and the Nature of Mind

The Buddhist ethical tradition, emerging from the Dharma of Siddhartha Gautama (c. 563–483 BCE), shares deep structural similarities with Thirukkural on several key principles — particularly compassion (karuna/arul), nonviolence (ahimsa/kollamai), and the relationship between mental purity and ethical action.

Buddhist Principle	Buddhist Teaching	Thirukkural Parallel	Key Difference
Karuna (Compassion)	Compassion for all sentient beings is a brahma-vihara (divine dwelling)	Arul (compassion/grace) is the central virtue (Kural 241-250)	Buddhism: compassion leads toward liberation. Thiruvalluvar: compassion enables engaged social and political life
Ahimsa (Non-harm)	Non-harm to all sentient beings; first precept	Kollamai (non-killing) as foundational (Kural 321-330)	Convergence is nearly complete here — both treat non-harm as the ethical foundation
Citta (Mind)	"Mind is the forerunner of all actions" (Dhammapada 1)	Mental purity is the foundation of all virtue (Kural 34)	Buddhism: purify mind to achieve liberation. Thiruvalluvar: purify mind to achieve virtuous social engagement
Anicca (Impermanence)	All conditioned phenomena are impermanent; clinging causes suffering	Nilayaamai: impermanence of all worldly things (Kural 331-340)	Buddhism: impermanence supports renunciation. Thiruvalluvar: impermanence supports ethical urgency
Sila (Ethical Conduct)	The first of the Three Trainings (sila, samadhi, prajna)	Aram: the first and foundational book of Thirukkural	Both: ethical conduct (sila/aram) is the prerequisite for all higher development

Chapter 48: Thirukkural and Modern Humanism

Universal Ethics, Human Rights, and Global Citizenship

Modern Humanism — the philosophical tradition that grounds ethics in human reason and human dignity rather than supernatural authority — finds in Thirukkural one of the ancient world's most congenial texts. The secular-universal character of Thiruvalluvar's ethics, its grounding of virtue in human flourishing rather than divine command, and its extension of moral concern beyond any single culture or religion make it a natural ally of contemporary humanist ethics.

Humanist Principle	Modern Formulation	Thirukkural Parallel	Kural
Human Dignity	Every person has inherent worth regardless of origin (UDHR Art. 1)	Compassion (arul) is owed to all; cruelty to any diminishes the human (Kural 241)	241
Reason over Dogma	Ethics must be grounded in reason, evidence, and human experience	Test all claims by reason before accepting (Kural 423)	423
Universal Ethics	Moral principles must apply equally to all humans regardless of identity	Sengol (justice) weighs all equally; partiality corrupts justice (Kural 541)	541
Human Flourishing	The goal of ethics is the full flourishing of human capacities	Aram → Porul → Inbam: the complete human life encompasses virtue, society, and love	1-1330
Global Citizenship	Moral community extends beyond nation, ethnicity, and religion	"yaaryaarkum" (for all, whoever they may be) in Kural 20	20
Pluralism	Multiple paths to the good life; tolerance of difference	Thirukkural's deliberate refusal to specify a single religious path	All

Chapter 49

Why Thirukkural Matters to Humanity

The Question That Demands an Answer

We live in 2026. The world has quantum computers, large language models, CRISPR gene editing, hypersonic weapons, and social media that can reach three billion people in seconds. We have mapped the human genome, landed rovers on Mars, and detected gravitational waves from colliding black holes a billion light-years away.

So why should we read Thirukkural? Why should a text written in seven-word Tamil verse two thousand years ago matter to a software engineer in Seoul, a policy maker in Brussels, a student in Lagos, a climate scientist in Boston, a parent in Mumbai?

This final chapter offers seven answers. Not arguments — but reasons grounded in human experience that no amount of technological progress has made obsolete.

I. Because the hardest questions have not been answered

We have solved many problems that tormented earlier generations. We have antibiotics, vaccines, anesthesia, and surgery. We have democratic institutions, international law, and human rights frameworks. We have smartphones, GPS, and the internet.

But the questions Thiruvalluvar asked remain unanswered — not because we haven't tried, but because they resist technological solution. How do we build leaders who will not abuse power? How do we create institutions that remain just over time? How do we love without possessiveness? How do we live with our own mortality? How do we resist the pull of easy cruelty when we can act with impunity?

These are not technical problems. They are human problems. And Thirukkural is a sustained, profound engagement with human problems.

II. Because it has survived two thousand years of testing

Any idea can sound plausible when it is new. The genuine test of an ethical idea is whether it survives contact with radically different historical circumstances — different technologies, different political systems, different economic arrangements, different crises.

Thirukkural has survived: the Roman Empire and its fall, the rise and decline of Islamic civilization, the Mughal Empire, European colonialism, the two World Wars, the Cold War, digital globalization. Through all of these cataclysms, readers in different continents have picked up this text and found it speaking directly to their situation.

This is not sentimentality. It is the strongest available evidence that Thirukkural addresses something real and permanent about human nature.

III. Because it transcends every sectarian boundary

One of the remarkable features of Thirukkural's 2,000-year history is that every major religious tradition — Hindu, Jain, Buddhist, Christian, Islamic, and secular humanist — has claimed it as consistent with their own values. Atheists appreciate it. Mystics venerate it. Rationalists cite it.

This is not because the text is vague. It is because Thiruvalluvar deliberately grounded his ethics in what is common to all human experience — the need for truth, the capacity for compassion, the structure of just governance, the experience of love — rather than in any particular metaphysical framework.

In an era of rising sectarianism, identity politics, and civilizational conflict, a text that belongs to everyone and has been adopted by everyone is a rare and precious resource.

IV. Because it is relevant to the AI Age

Artificial intelligence is the defining technological development of our era. It will reshape how we work, how we make decisions, how we allocate resources, and how we understand ourselves. The ethical questions it raises — about fairness, accountability, truth, human dignity, and the limits of optimization — are among the most urgent of our time.

Thirukkural does not contain a chapter on AI. But it contains something more fundamental: a framework for thinking about what makes human systems — whether those systems are governments, markets, families, or AI algorithms — just or unjust. The values required for ethical AI are not technical innovations. They are ancient human values: truth-telling, non-harm, accountability, justice, and human welfare as the ultimate criterion. All of these are articulated in Thirukkural with greater depth than in most contemporary AI ethics frameworks.

V. Because the climate crisis demands its wisdom

We are living through the first planetary crisis in human history — a crisis caused by human action and requiring human transformation to address. The IPCC tells us we have a narrow window to avoid the most catastrophic climate outcomes. What it cannot tell us is how to achieve the social and political transformation required.

Thirukkural can contribute. Its environmental ethics — grounded in the insight that rain (the water cycle) is sacred, that nature is the precondition of all human civilization, that "yaaryaarkum" (all living beings) have claims on our ethical attention — provides a philosophical foundation for climate action that goes deeper than economics or policy.

We have enough climate science. What we lack is the moral imagination to act on it. Thirukkural can help cultivate that imagination.

VI. Because democracy needs its insights

Liberal democracy is under pressure worldwide — from authoritarian governments externally and from erosion of civic virtue internally. The institutions of democracy (free elections, independent judiciary, free press, civil society) are necessary but not sufficient. Democratic institutions require democratic citizens — people who value truth, who can tolerate disagreement, who hold power accountable, who care about justice even when they are not the ones being wronged.

Thirukkural's treatment of justice, of the duty of rulers to the ruled, of the corruption that follows when power is held without accountability — these are not ancient curiosities. They are urgent contemporary needs. The text reminds us that the quality of governance depends ultimately on the character of the governed, not just the governed's institutions.

VII. Because its final word is love

Thiruvalluvar could have ended his great work with ethics. He could have ended it with governance. He could have ended it with philosophical wisdom. He ended it with love — 250 kurals on the experience of human connection, longing, union, and the joy that makes life worth living.

This is not a concession to sentimentality. It is a philosophical position of the highest order: that the ethical life and the political life, however important, do not constitute the fullness of human existence. The fullness requires love — the willingness to be deeply known and to deeply know another, to be changed by connection, to find that another person's existence matters more than one's own convenience.

In an age of increasing social atomization, loneliness epidemics, digital pseudo-connection, and the instrumentalization of human relationships, Thiruvalluvar's insistence that love is the crown of the good life is more radical, and more necessary, than it has ever been.

> *"The greatness of Thirukkural is not that it belongs to Tamil civilization. The greatness of Thirukkural is that it transcends Tamil civilization and speaks to humanity itself. It is not Tamil literature. It is human literature — written in Tamil."*
>
> **— Dr. Perumal Pugazhendhi**

The Final Thesis

For two thousand years, Thiruvalluvar has been asking us the same questions. Not because he did not know the answers — but because each generation must find them anew, in its own circumstances, against its own temptations.

The questions are: How will you live? How will you govern? Who will you love? What will you leave behind?

No technology answers these questions. No algorithm resolves them. They are answered — imperfectly, partially, with backsliding and renewal — by human beings who choose, against all odds and temptations, to be good.

Thiruvalluvar wrote for those people. He wrote for us.

நலனோடு வாழுங்கள். நேர்மையோடு ஆளுங்கள். ஆழமாக காதலியுங்கள்.

Live with goodness. Govern with honesty. Love deeply.

Appendix I: The Complete 133 Chapters of Thirukkural

அறம் — Aram: Chapters 1–38

No.	Tamil Title	English	Kurals
1	கடவுள் வாழ்த்து	In Praise of God	1–10
2	வான் சிறப்பு	The Excellence of Rain	11–20
3	நீத்தார் பெருமை	The Greatness of Ascetics	21–30
4	அறன் வலியுறுத்தல	The Power of Virtue	31–40
5	இல்வாழ்க்கை	Domestic Life	41–50
6	வாழ்க்கைத் துணை நலம	The Worth of a Good Companion	51–60
7	மக்கட்பேறு	Children	61–70
8	அன்புடைமை	The Nature of Love	71–80
9	விருந்தோம்பல்	Hospitality	81–90
10	இனியவை கூறல்	Speaking Pleasantly	91–100
11	செய்ந்நன்றி அறிதல	Gratitude	101–110
12	நடுவு நிலைமை	Impartiality	111–120
13	அடக்கமுடைமை	Self-Discipline	121–130
14	ஒழுக்கமுடைமை	Ethical Conduct	131–140
15	பிறனில் விழையாமை	Non-Coveting of Others' Spouses	141–150
16	பொறையுடைமை	Patience	151–160
17	அழுக்காறாமை	Non-Envy	161–170
18	வெஃகாமை	Non-Greed	171–180
19	புறங்கூறாமை	Non-Gossip	181–190
20	பயனில சொல்லாமை	Avoiding Vain Words	191–200
21	தீவினையச்சம்	Fear of Evil Deeds	201–210
22	ஒப்புரவு அறிதல்	Knowing What Is Fitting	211–220
23	ஈகை	Generosity	221–230
24	புகழ்	Fame	231–240

25	அருளுடைமை	Compassion	241–250
26	புலால் மறுத்தல்	Abstaining from Meat	251–260
27	தவம்	Austerity	261–270
28	கூடாவொழுக்கம்	Hypocrisy	271–280
29	கள்ளாமை	Non-Stealing	281–290
30	வாய்மை	Truth	291–300
31	வெகுளாமை	Non-Anger	301–310
32	இன்னா செய்யாமை	Non-Harm	311–320
33	கொல்லாமை	Nonviolence	321–330
34	நிலையாமை	Impermanence	331–340
35	துறவு	Renunciation	341–350
36	மெய்யுணர்தல்	Knowing Truth	351–360
37	அவாவறுத்தல்	Mastering Desire	361–370
38	ஊழ்	Fate	371–380

Appendix II: Timeline — Thiruvalluvar and Major Historical Events

This appendix places the life and work of Thiruvalluvar within the broader context of South Asian and world history. Although scholars continue to debate the precise date of Thiruvalluvar, most studies place him between the last centuries BCE and the early centuries CE.

Date/Period	Major Historical Event
6th–5th century BCE	Lifetime of Gautama Buddha
4th century BCE	Alexander's invasion of northwestern India
322 BCE	Foundation of the Mauryan Empire
3rd century BCE	Reign of Emperor Ashoka and his inscriptions
3rd–1st centuries BCE	Growth and consolidation of early Tamil (Sangam) society
31 BCE	Traditional date adopted for the beginning of the Thiruvalluvar Era (widely used in Tamil scholarship and public life)
1st century BCE – 1st century CE	Probable period during which the *Tirukkural* was composed
1st century CE	Peak of maritime trade between Tamilakam and the Roman Empire
2nd century CE	Approximate period associated with the composition of *Silappathikaram* and *Manimekalai*
5th–6th centuries CE	Earliest known references and wider circulation of the *Tirukkural*
10th–13th centuries CE	Emergence of major commentators, including Parimelazhagar
20th century CE	Broad adoption of the Thiruvalluvar Era in education, scholarship, and public administration in Tamil Nadu

Historical Significance

Although Thiruvalluvar's exact date remains uncertain, linguistic evidence, social references within the *Tirukkural*, its non-sectarian ethical framework, and its relationship to Sangam literature suggest that he belonged to the formative period of classical Tamil civilization. His work reflects a mature urban and commercial society, sophisticated political thought, and a universal ethical vision that transcended religious boundaries.

Viewed against the backdrop of world history, Thiruvalluvar appears not merely as a Tamil poet but as one of the great moral philosophers of the ancient world, whose teachings emerged during a period marked by expanding trade networks, cultural exchange, and significant intellectual developments across Asia and the Mediterranean. The *Tirukkural* remains one of the most enduring contributions of Tamil civilization to global ethical thought.

Appendix III: Key Tamil Ethical Terms — Comprehensive Glossary

Tamil	Transliteration	English	Full Semantic Range
அறம்	Aram	Virtue/Duty	righteousness, morality, justice, ethical life, dharma
பொருள்	Porul	Material/Governance	wealth, statecraft, social order, public affairs
இன்பம்	Inbam	Love/Joy	pleasure, happiness, love, emotional fulfillment
அருள்	Arul	Compassion/Grace	divine compassion, human kindness, benevolent love
அன்பு	Anbu	Affection/Love	love, family bonds, social connection
ஒழுக்கம்	Ozhukkam	Conduct/Discipline	ethical behavior, personal discipline, social propriety
வாய்மை	Vaymai	Truthfulness	language honesty, alignment with reality, trustworthiness
அடக்கம்	Adakkam	Self-Control	restraint, emotional regulation, mastery of desire
அறிவு	Arivu	Wisdom	knowledge, understanding, clarity, practical intelligence
நேர்மை	Nermai	Integrity	directness, honesty, ethical straightforwardness
தவம்	Thavam	Austerity	spiritual discipline, ascetic practice, self-mortification
ஈகை	Eekai	Generosity	charity, free giving, magnanimity
புகழ்	Pugazh	Fame	good reputation, glory, honorable legacy
செங்கோல்	Sengol	Justice/Scepter	the balanced scepter of impartial justice
தூது	Thoodhu	Diplomacy	ambassadorship, the art of ethical representation
நட்பு	Natpu	Friendship	true friendship, enduring bond, alliance in adversity
காதல்	Kaadal	Love (romantic)	passionate love, longing, the experience of deep connection
வாழ்க்கை	Vaazkhkai	Life/Living	the art and practice of a fully human life

Appendix IV: Thirukkural for the 21st Century

Selected Kurals for Contemporary Domains

Domain	Kural(s)	Core Principle	Application
Artificial Intelligence	291, 423, 467, 541, 571	Truth, tested reason, precaution, justice, human welfare	AI transparency, fairness testing, safety-first development, human-centered design
Climate Action	11, 18, 20, 1033	Rain as sacred, nature precedes culture, all beings depend on water	Water conservation policy, regenerative agriculture, planetary boundaries framework
Medical Ethics	34, 241, 321	Mental purity, compassion, non-harm	Informed consent, palliative care ethics, healthcare justice
Legal Systems	541, 544, 547, 550	Law grounded in ethics, scepter of justice, balanced weighing	Rule of law vs. rule by law; judicial impartiality; constitutional review
Diplomacy	681, 683, 687, 690	Love+knowledge+character, timing+duty+context, fearless truth, learning+courage	Diplomatic training; multilateral negotiations; truth-telling in foreign policy
Entrepreneurship	467, 659, 671, 754	Careful action, ethical wealth, long-term thinking, genuine partnership	Ethical startup culture; stakeholder commitment; sustainable business models
Education	391, 400, 423	Learn without residue, live accordingly; imperishable knowledge; test by reason	Deep learning pedagogy; lifelong learning; epistemic humility in curricula
Global Citizenship	20, 241, 321	All beings matter; compassion as greatest wealth; nonviolence as foundation	Human rights education; animal welfare; environmental responsibility

Appendix V: Study Guide for Students and Researchers

Beginner's Reading Path

1. Begin with the Preface and Introduction to establish historical and philosophical context.
2. Read Chapters 1–3 (Part I) on Thiruvalluvar's life and ancient Tamil society.
3. Select 20–30 kurals from the 100 key kurals list, covering Aram, Porul, and Inbam.
4. Compare at least two translations for each kural you study.
5. Keep a reflection journal: "How does this kural apply to my life today?"

Intermediate Study Path

6. Read the full Aram section (Chapters 7–22) with original Tamil where possible.
7. Study the Porul chapters (23–29) with focus on governance and leadership applications.
8. Engage with Inbam (Chapters 30–33) as psychological and philosophical study.
9. Read Chapter 34 (Comparative Philosophy) alongside primary texts of Aristotle, Confucius, and Stoics.
10. Write comparative essays connecting Thirukkural to contemporary ethical debates.

Advanced Research Path

11. Engage with the original Tamil using the Tamil Lexicon (University of Madras) and classical grammar.
12. Study all four classical commentaries: Manakkudavar, Parimelazhagar, Kalingar, Parithiyar.
13. Read Kamil Zvelebil on Tamil Literature and A.K. Ramanujan on Sangam poetry for cultural context.
14. Research Keeladi excavation reports (ASI Publications) for archaeological context.
15. Conduct original comparative research connecting Thirukkural to your specific field of expertise.

Bibliography — Primary, Secondary, and Modern Sources

Primary Sources: Classical Tamil Texts

- Thiruvalluvar. Thirukkural. Various editions. Original Tamil text (1st c. BCE–2nd c. CE).
- Parimelazhagar. Parimelazhagar Urai (Commentary on Thirukkural). 13th century CE.
- Manakkudavar. Manakkudavar Urai (Commentary on Thirukkural). 9th–10th century CE.
- Kalingar. Kalingar Urai (Commentary on Thirukkural). 11th–12th century CE.
- Parithiyar. Parithiyar Urai (Commentary on Thirukkural). 10th–11th century CE.
- Tolkappiyam. Ancient Tamil grammar text. Tolkappiyar (c. 100 BCE–200 CE).
- Purananuru. Sangam anthology of classical Tamil poetry. Various authors (c. 100–300 CE).
- Akananuru. Sangam anthology of love poetry. Various authors (c. 100–300 CE).
- Silappathikaram. Ilango Adigal (c. 2nd–5th century CE).
- Manimekalai. Chithalai Chathanar (c. 2nd–5th century CE).

Translations of Thirukkural

- Pope, G.U. The Sacred Kurral of Tiruvalluvar Nayanar. Oxford: Clarendon Press, 1886.
- Sundaram, P.S. The Kural. New Delhi: Penguin Books India, 1990.
- Ramachandran, T.N. Thirukkural: English Translation and Commentary. Chennai: Tiruvalluvar Karyal, 1972.
- Pruiksma, Thomas. The Thirukkural: A New Translation. New Delhi: Rupa Publications, 2014.

Archaeology and History

- Archaeological Survey of India (ASI). Keeladi Excavation Reports. Vols. I–VIII. Chennai, 2015–2023.
- Tamil Nadu State Archaeology Department. Annual Reports on Archaeological Findings in Tamilnadu.
- Soundararajan, K.V. "Arikamedu: An Indo-Roman Trading Station." Ancient India 2 (1945): 15–26.
- Subrahmanian, N. Sangam Polity. Madurai: Ennes Publications, 1966.

Classical Philosophy — Primary Sources

- Aristotle. Nicomachean Ethics. Trans. W.D. Ross. Oxford: Oxford University Press, 1998.
- Aristotle. Politics. Trans. C.D.C. Reeve. Indianapolis: Hackett, 1998.
- Confucius. The Analects. Trans. D.C. Lau. London: Penguin Classics, 1979.
- Marcus Aurelius. Meditations. Trans. Gregory Hays. New York: Modern Library, 2002.

- Epictetus. Discourses and Selected Writings. Trans. Robert Dobbin. London: Penguin Classics, 2008.
- Seneca. Letters on Ethics. Trans. Margaret Graver. Chicago: University of Chicago Press, 2015.
- Dhammapada. Trans. Acharya Buddharakkhita. Sri Lanka: Buddhist Publication Society, 1985.

Tamil Studies — Secondary Sources

- Zvelebil, Kamil V. Tamil Literature. Wiesbaden: Otto Harrassowitz, 1974.
- Ramanujan, A.K. Poems of Love and War: From the Eight Anthologies. New York: Columbia University Press, 1985.
- Cutler, Norman. Songs of Experience: The Poetics of Tamil Devotion. Bloomington: Indiana University Press, 1987.
- Hart, George L. The Poems of Ancient Tamil. Berkeley: University of California Press, 1975.
- University of Madras. Tamil Lexicon. Madras: University of Madras, 1924–1936.

Modern Research — Governance, Ethics, Philosophy

- Rawls, John. A Theory of Justice. Cambridge: Harvard University Press, 1971.
- Nussbaum, Martha C. Creating Capabilities: The Human Development Approach. Cambridge: Harvard University Press, 2011.
- Sen, Amartya. The Idea of Justice. Cambridge: Harvard University Press, 2009.
- Haidt, Jonathan. The Righteous Mind. New York: Pantheon Books, 2012.
- Nye, Joseph S. Soft Power: The Means to Success in World Politics. New York: Public Affairs, 2004.
- Weber, Max. Economy and Society. Berkeley: University of California Press, 1978 [1922].
- Tyler, Tom R. Why People Obey the Law. Princeton: Princeton University Press, 2006.

AI Ethics and Technology

- Floridi, Luciano, et al. "An Ethical Framework for a Good AI Society." Minds and Machines 28 (2018): 689–707.
- Jobin, Anna, Marcello Ienca, and Effy Vayena. "The Global Landscape of AI Ethics Guidelines." Nature Machine Intelligence 1 (2019): 389–399.
- Russell, Stuart. Human Compatible: Artificial Intelligence and the Problem of Control. New York: Viking, 2019.
- European Union. Artificial Intelligence Act. Brussels: European Parliament, 2024.
- Dafoe, Allan. "AI Governance: A Research Agenda." Future of Humanity Institute, University of Oxford, 2018.

Environment and Sustainability

- IPCC. Climate Change 2022: Impacts, Adaptation and Vulnerability. Sixth Assessment Report. Geneva: IPCC, 2022.
- Rockström, Johan, et al. "A Safe Operating Space for Humanity." Nature 461 (2009): 472–475.
- Raworth, Kate. Doughnut Economics: Seven Ways to Think Like a 21st-Century Economist. London: Random House, 2017.
- Daly, Herman. Beyond Growth: The Economics of Sustainable Development. Boston: Beacon Press, 1996.
- Leopold, Aldo. A Sand County Almanac. Oxford: Oxford University Press, 1949.

Psychology and Neuroscience

- Bowlby, John. Attachment and Loss. 3 vols. New York: Basic Books, 1969–1980.
- Gottman, John M. Why Marriages Succeed or Fail. New York: Simon & Schuster, 1994.
- Fisher, Helen. Why We Love: The Nature and Chemistry of Romantic Love. New York: Henry Holt, 2004.
- Haidt, Jonathan. The Righteous Mind: Why Good People Are Divided by Politics and Religion. New York: Pantheon, 2012.
- Bandura, Albert. "Moral Disengagement in the Perpetration of Inhumanities." Personality and Social Psychology Review 3(3) (1999): 193–209.

United Nations and International Policy

- United Nations. Universal Declaration of Human Rights. New York: UN, 1948.
- United Nations. Transforming Our World: The 2030 Agenda for Sustainable Development. New York: UN, 2015.
- UNESCO. Convention Concerning the Protection of the World Cultural and Natural Heritage. Paris: UNESCO, 1972.

About the Author

Dr. Perumal Pugazhendhi, Ph.D., is a scientist, inventor, and multidisciplinary researcher with over forty years of experience in energy technologies, materials science, electrochemical systems, nanotechnology, and applied engineering research. He has led and contributed to research and development projects supported by NASA, the U.S. Department of Energy, the U.S. Department of Defense, the U.S. Air Force, and the U.S. Army.

This book continues his broader intellectual engagement with Tamil civilization and South Asian cultural history, bringing scientific rigor and global perspective to one of the world's greatest ethical texts. His unique position — a scientist deeply rooted in Tamil culture and engaged with global intellectual traditions — gives this study its distinctive voice: both analytically rigorous and personally passionate about the timeless wisdom of Thiruvalluvar.

Dr. Pugazhendhi believes that Thirukkural is not Tamil literature. It is human literature, written in Tamil — and its time has come for the world.

Disclaimer

This book is intended for educational, literary, and scholarly purposes. The interpretations, analyses, and comparisons presented herein reflect the author's research and understanding of the *Thirukkural* and should not be regarded as the only or definitive interpretation. While every effort has been made to ensure accuracy, readers are encouraged to consult the original text, classical commentaries, and other scholarly works for further study. Any errors or omissions are solely the responsibility of the author

— End of Thirukkural: Time, Civilization, and Humanity —

நலனோடு வாழுங்கள். நேர்மையோடு ஆளுங்கள். ஆழமாக காதலியுங்கள்.

Live with goodness. Govern with honesty. Love deeply.

www.ingramcontent.com/pod-product-compliance
Lightning Source LLC
LaVergne TN
LVRC090740061126
851857LV00007B/36

* 9 7 9 8 2 5 6 1 1 8 5 9 4 *